The Original Trivia Treasury

1,001 Questions for Competitive Play

The Original Trivia Treasury

1,001 Questions for Competitive Play

R. Wayne Schmittberger

John Wiley & Sons, Inc.

New York • Chichester • Brisbane • Toronto • Singapore

Library of Congress Cataloging-in-Publication Data

Schmittberger, R. Wayne, 1949–
    The original trivia treasury: 1001 questions for competitive
  play / by Wayne Schmittberger
        p.   cm.
    ISBN 0-471-52759-9
    1. Questions and answers.   I. Title.
  AG195.S33   1991
031.02--dc20   90-42285
                                                      CIP

Printed in the United States of America

Contents

Preface

For most people, trivia games are played just for fun. I enjoy them too, but often my interest is more than casual. As a longtime creator of trivia games and quizzes, I am always trying to learn more about what kinds of questions people enjoy most, and what kinds of game rules seem to work best. Two of my observations helped give me the idea for this book.

First, I noticed that in trivia board games, most people like answering the questions more than moving their tokens around the board. I have often seen people dispense with the board entirely in a game such as Trivial Pursuit. They sit back on a sofa, or outdoors on a lounge chair or on a beach (where a board isn't all that practical to set up, anyway), and simply take turns asking each other questions from the game cards.

Second, I concluded that although multiple choice questions were rarely found in trivia games, they have several advantages over objective, or "fill-in-the-blank," questions. The same applies to true-false questions, which are essentially multiple choice questions with just two possible answers. The most important advantages of the multiple choice and true-false formats are:

- Every player has a fighting chance on every question, even if it asks about the player's weakest subject.

- Questions can be asked that are fun to guess at, even though no one can reasonably be expected to know the exact answer—e.g., "How many automobiles were on the road in 1900?"

- No arguments ever arise about whether to accept an answer that is incomplete or only partly right.

Looking for facts that were unusual and intriguing, I began collecting questions even before I knew exactly what I was going to do with them. My sources include countless newspapers, magazines, reference books, and primary sources ranging from movie videotapes to product labels. To make the gameplay as competitive and exciting as possible, I deliberately included many questions on which I expect players to have to guess—so don't get worried if you find you're doing a lot of just that. Most of the questions are my own, but I want to express sincere thanks to Henry Hook, Scott Marley, Stephanie Spadaccini, and John Strother for their question contributions, which have helped broaden the scope of this book.

I've tried to design the games to suit a wide variety of tastes, and to accommodate any number of players. To play these games, all you need is this book, and (in some cases) paper and pencil to keep score. As a result, the games can be played anywhere—outdoors, traveling, or in your living room—and they don't require any setting up.

Still, some of you may prefer just to read the questions and take turns answering them. My goal was to create a book that could be enjoyed in many different ways, and to leave the ways you choose to enjoy it entirely up to you.

— R.W.S.

Introduction

How to Use This Book

As its title implies, this book contains not only trivia questions but also rules for games that can be played using those questions.

Some readers may prefer to skip the game rules in Chapter 1, and immediately start reading and trying to answer the questions in Chapters 2-11. Others may want to use the questions in the book as supplements for their favorite trivia board games. (Chapters 3-8, containing questions in six different categories, are especially useful for this purpose, since many trivia board games use six question categories.)

But for readers who are willing to try some new—and, I think, exciting—kinds of entertainment and challenge, the games in Chapter 1 offer a variety of choices. There are games suitable for large groups, small groups, and even solitaire play. All are quick and easy to learn, and none require any materials other than this book, and paper and pencil for keeping score.

The game that's best for you depends on how many players you want to include, and also on your personal taste. You may wish to read through the rules to all seven games before choosing one—or, you can just try them all out, one at a time, until you find your favorite.

How the Book Is Organized

Chapter 1 contains rules for seven competitive games, as well as three solitaire variations. The rest of the book consists of questions (Chapters 2-11) and their answers (in the back of the book). Questions are grouped in different ways in different chapters, for more convenient use in different kinds of games.

All questions in this book have one of three formats. Each format corresponds to a particular point value:

1.   true-false (1-point questions)

2.   multiple choice with three possible answers (2-point questions)

3.   multiple choice with four possible answers (3-point questions)

These point values are not used in every game; but for convenience, the different question formats will be referred to as "1-point," "2-point," and "3-point" throughout the book, even when discussing games in which point values do not matter.

The question chapters consist of the following:

- Chapter 2 contains 10 sets of 25 questions each. Each set contains eight questions of each format, plus one extra 3-point question. Questions are of the "general knowledge" variety—that is, different subjects are covered, and are mixed together at random.

- Chapters 3-8 each contain 75 questions related to a particular subject or subjects. Within each chapter, 25 questions are 1-pointers, 25 are 2-pointers, and 25 are 3-pointers. The chapter titles indicate the subjects covered: Entertainment, Literature, and Art; Geography and Sightseeing; History and Demographics; Science and Nature; Sports and Games; and Potpourri (general knowledge, but with an emphasis on questions that do not clearly fit into one of the other chapters' categories).

- Chapter 9 contains 100 1-point questions (general knowledge).

- Chapter 10 contains 100 2-point questions (general knowledge).

- Chapter 11 contains 101 3-point questions (general knowledge).

Looking Up the Answers

One of the drawbacks of some quiz books is that a reader who is looking up the answer to one question may accidentally see the answer to the next question. This problem can be serious when the questions are being used to play games, as in this book.

To avoid this situation, answers to each chapter's questions have been rearranged, so that they appear in an order different from the order of the questions—though each chapter's answers are still grouped together.

To find the answer to a particular question, use the number that appears in brackets at the end of each question. That's the number of the question's answer, as it appears in the back of the book.

For example, at the end of question 2.1, which is the first question in Chapter 2, the number "[36]" appears. That means that answer number 36, in the portion of the answers that is devoted to Chapter 2, will be the answer to question 2.1. (When looking up an answer, make sure you are in the answer section that goes with the chapter where the question is. The page where each chapter's answers begin is listed both in the Table of Contents and on the first page of each chapter.)

This system is not designed to prevent deliberate cheating, though it will make it more difficult. But cheating is rare in games of this sort. Players participate not because they have anything important at stake, but because they just want to have fun—while learning some amusing facts along the way.

Chapter 1

Game Rules

General Rules

Rules to seven competitive games, plus three solitaire variations, appear below. Before reading the different games' rules, though, players should familiarize themselves with these general rules, which apply to all the games.

1. Players decide, in any convenient fashion, who will have the first turn. Players might draw straws, or let the loser of the previous game go first, or give the honor to whichever player will be the next to celebrate a birthday.

2. Each player, in turn, answers one or more questions, depending on which game is being played. When a player's turn is over, the turn passes clockwise around the table.

3. When a question is to be answered, it is read aloud by any player (preferably, by one of the other players—though this is not necessary). The player who reads the question is also responsible for looking up the answer and announcing it.

Team Play

The most players listed for any game is six. Most of these games could be played with more people, but each player would then have to wait a long time between turns. And multi-player versions of the strictly two-player games (Challenge Trivia and Strikeout) could be improvised, but would require adding complicated rules to manage the player interaction.

By grouping players into teams, though, it is possible to play any of these games with just about any number of players. Teams can operate in either of two ways, as the players prefer:

1. In "rotation" team play, players on a team take turns answering a question whenever it is the team's turn. No consultation among teammates is allowed.

2. In "consultation" team play, each team should choose one of its members as "team captain." When the team is read a question, members may consult with one another before answering. When two or more members disagree, the captain will decide which answer a team will give. The captain will also resolve any other disagreements by teammates, such as whether or not to challenge in "Challenge Trivia" (Game Five).

Solitaire Play

Three of the games (First to Finish, Boxing, and Double or Nothing) have solitaire versions. Rules for each appear at the end of the rules for the corresponding competitive game.

Hints for Easier Play

1. When you will be referring repeatedly to a certain chapter's answers during a game, mark the location of the answers with a bookmark.

2. Keep a pencil handy to check off the last question answered on any page. That way, no questions will be skipped later on, and unused questions can be identified for later use in other games.

3. To share the task of reading questions equally, players may wish to adopt a rule that questions are always asked by the player to the left of the one who will be answering. An alternative, which reduces the need to pass the book from player to player as often, is to have one player read all the questions for an entire round— even his or her own question(s). After the round (i.e., after each player has taken one turn), another player takes over the job.

4. To help you choose a game, the Quick Reference Chart on page 16 shows the number of players that are best for each game, which games have solitaire versions, and which question sets go with which rules.

Game One: First to Finish

Number of players: 2-4
Questions to use: Chapter 2

Rules

1. Each player chooses a different Question Set from Chapter 2.

2. The first player tries to answer the first question in his or her set.
   (i) On a correct answer, the player takes another turn by trying the next question in the set.
   (ii) On an incorrect answer, the player's turn ends.

3. When a player answers the last question in his or her set, one of two things happens:
   (i) If the player answers the final question correctly, he or she wins the game.
   (ii) If the player answers the final question incorrectly, he or she still may win—but first, every other player, in order, gets to take one more turn. During this final

round, if a player reaches the last question in his or her question set, and answers that question correctly, he or she is the winner. If no one is able to accomplish this, the first player to have reached the end of the question set wins after all.

Solitaire Variation

Choose a question set from Chapter 2, and see how many turns it takes you to reach the end, following the same rules as above. Missing the final question adds one turn to your total. If you get through the set in 12 or fewer turns, you win. If it takes you 13-15 turns, you get credit for a draw. If it takes you more than 15 turns, you lose.

Game Two: Boxing

Number of players: 2-3
Questions Used: Chapters 3-8

Rules

1. Players copy this grid. (Just one copy is needed, which all players will share.)

	1-point questions	2-point questions	3-point questions
Entertainment, Literature, and Art			
Geography and Sightseeing			
History and Demographics			
Science and Nature			
Sports and Games			
Potpourri			

Each box in the grid corresponds to a particular question format (listed above the box) and a particular category (listed to the left of the box).

2. In turn, a player chooses one of the 18 boxes in the grid, and answers a question of the format and category corresponding to the box.

3. If a player gives a correct answer, the player puts his or her initials in the box, and takes another turn—again choosing a box and answering a question of the appropriate category and format.

4. If a player gives an incorrect answer, the turn passes to the next player.

5. A player may not choose a box that already contains someone's initials.

6. When initials have been placed in all 18 boxes, the game is over. The winner is the player with initials in the most boxes. If there is a tie, players add up the point values of the boxes with their initials (1 point for each box in the 1-point column, 2 points for each 2-point box, 3 points for each 3-point box), and the player with the most points wins.

Strategy

Deciding what box to choose next is not as simple as choosing all the easy questions first, since most players will know certain categories better than others, and tiebreaking rules favor the harder question boxes. In a game where both players know one subject well, it is important to try to get initials in those boxes first. But if one player knows a category well, and the opponent doesn't, the player doesn't need to rush to answer questions in that category, since the opponent will probably avoid it anyway.

Solitaire Variation

As in the competitive version, the player chooses a box in the grid and answers a question of the corresponding category and format. On a correct answer, the player places his or her initials in the box. On an incorrect answer, however, the player places an "X" in the box. When the grid is full, the outcome is determined as in the regular game—except that instead of a real opponent, the player is competing against an imaginary player "X."

Game Three: Checkout

Number of players: 2-6
Questions Used: Chapters 3-8

Rules

1. The same kind of grid is used as in Boxing, except that this time, each player needs his or her own copy of the grid.

	1-point questions	2-point questions	3-point questions
Entertainment, Literature, and Art			
Geography and Sightseeing			
History and Demographics			
Science and Nature			
Sports and Games			
Potpourri			

2. Each player, in turn, chooses a question category and format, and tries to answer a question of that kind.
   (i) On giving a correct answer, the player checks the appropriate box on his or her grid. The player then takes another turn.

(ii) If the player gives an incorrect answer, his or her turn ends.

3. If a player gets checks in all the boxes of any row or column, he or she announces "Checkout" to the other players. The other players, on their own grids, must then write a "0" in each empty box they still have in that row or column.

Example: Player A has a check in the 2-point column of the Potpourri row, but not in the 1-point or 3-point columns. Player B then gets checks in all three boxes of his Potpourri row, and calls "Checkout." Player A must then put zeroes in the 1-point and 3-point boxes in that row, and can no longer try questions of those kinds.

---

4. A player may not call "Checkout" for a row or column in which he or she has any zeroes, even if all the other boxes in it are checked.

5. Players must keep their grids in plain view, and may study each others' grids before choosing their questions each turn.

6. When one player's grid is completely full—either of checks, zeroes, or (most likely) both—the game ends. Players then count their check marks, and the player with the most wins. If there is a tie, players add up the point values of the boxes they have checked (1 point for each box checked in the 1-point column, 2 points for each 2-point box checked, 3 points for each 3-point box checked), and the player with the most points wins.

Game Four: Twenty-One

Number of players: 2-6
Questions to use: Chapters 9-11

Rules

1. Players take turns answering one question per turn. The question format changes each round. That is, each player answers a 1-point question, then each answers a 2-point question, then a 3-point question; then back to a 1-pointer, and so on.

2. For giving a correct answer, players score—naturally enough—1 point for a 1-point question, 2 points for a 2-point question, and 3 points for a 3-point question.

3. A player loses 1 point for each incorrect answer, regardless of the question type.

4. The first player to reach 21 points is the winner—*provided* that all the other players have had the same number of turns as the winner. Players who have had one fewer turn are entitled to finish the round (unless they are too far behind for the extra question to help them catch up).

Note: The winning total may be changed to shorten or lengthen playing time. In games with four or more players, a winning total of 15 is recommended.

---

5. If two or more players are tied at a total of 21 or more, the game enters a "sudden death" phase. Play continues as before, but only includes the players who were tied for the lead. Each time a round ends, any player who is no longer

tied for the lead is eliminated, until only one winner remains.

6. (Optional) To avoid the 1-point penalty, a player who does not know the answer, and does not wish to guess, may "pass" after hearing the question. The question then goes to the next player. (But if the next player was due to start a round with a different question format, the question is saved until its format comes up again.) If all players pass a particular question, they go on to the next question.

Note: This scoring system is mathematically balanced so that a random guesser will get an average of 0 points on each question format. For example, a random guesser would typically get one right and two wrong in a set of three 2-point questions; and his or her score for those three questions would be $2 - 1 - 1 = 0$.

Game Five: Challenge Trivia

Number of players: 2 (or 2 teams)
Questions Used: Chapters 9-11

Rules

This game is played the same way as Twenty-One (Game Four, above), except for the following.

1. The game is played by only two players (or two teams).

2. After a player gives an answer to a question, but before the answer is looked up in the book, the opponent may say "Challenge" if he or she thinks the answer given by the player is incorrect.

3. The challenging player then gives his or her own answer to the question.

4. When the answer is looked up, points are scored as follows:
    (i)   If the player's original answer was correct, he or she earns double the usual number of points for that question format. That is, instead of earning 1 point for a 1-point question, 2 for a 2-point question, and 3 for a 3-point question (which would be the case if the player's correct answer went unchallenged), the player earns 2 points for a 1-point question, 4 for a 2-point question, and 6 for a 3-point question. The challenger does not lose any points.
    (ii) If the challenger's answer was correct, the challenger earns 1 point if the question was a 1-pointer, 2 if it was a 2-pointer, and 3 if it was a 3-pointer. In addition, the player loses a point, as usual, for giving an incorrect answer.
    (iii) If both the player and the challenger give incorrect answers, the challenger loses a point, but the player does not.

5. The winner is the first player to reach 31 points.

Game Six:
Double or Nothing

Number of players: 2-6
Questions Used: Chapters 9-11

Rules

In this game of nerve, players must decide how much to bet on themselves.

1. Question formats rotate each round, as in Twenty-One (Game Four, above).

2. Players take turns answering at least one question per turn.

3. If a player answers a question correctly, he or she has two options:
    (i) End the turn, and take whatever points the question was worth (1, 2, or 3, depending on the format); or
    (ii) Answer another question of the same format.
         If the player chooses option (ii), and gives another correct answer, the player's score for that turn doubles. The player then has the same two options—to end the turn and take the points earned so far, or to try another question in an attempt to again double his or her points for that turn. But if the player gives an incorrect answer, he or she gets no points for that round, and his or her turn ends. (The player does not lose any points earned in previous rounds.)

4. Play continues until one player reaches a winning point total of 50 points.

Here's an example of how a two-player game might start. Player A answers a 1-point question correctly. Player A decides to answer a second 1-point question, and gets that one right, too, doubling his score to 2 points. Then he tries a third 1-point question, and gets it right as well, doubling his score to 4. Satisfied, he decides to end his turn.

Player B answers a 1-point question correctly. B then tries a second 1-pointer, but gets it wrong—wiping out the point she had earned with the first question, and ending the round with a score of zero.

The second round uses 2-point questions. Player A gets his first question right, earning 2 points. Having a lead, with a two-round total now of 6 points, he decides to play conservatively, and he chooses to end his turn.

Player B now tries a 2-point question, and gets it right, for 2 points. She decides to answer another question, which she also gets right, doubling her total to 4. Then she answers another question and gets it right, redoubling her total to 8. Now in the lead, she decides to end her turn.

Solitaire Variation

Using the same rules as the competitive game, a player has 10 turns in which to score at least 50 points. If this goal proves too hard or too easy for a player to achieve, he or she can simply play each game with the goal of breaking his or her own personal high score.

Game Seven: Strikeout

Number of players: 2 (or two teams)
Questions Used: All (Chapters 2-11)

Rules

1. In turn, a player announces that he or she can answer one, two, or three questions in a row correctly. The player must also specify the format and chapter of each question he or she will try to answer. For example, a player might say,

"I'll answer a 1-pointer and a 2-pointer, both in the Sports and Games category" (meaning Chapter 7). Or he might say, "I'll answer three 2-point questions in a row from Chapter 5." He then tries to do what he has promised.

2. If the player succeeds in giving all correct answers, the opponent must try to do the same. If the opponent fails, the opponent gets one strike. If the player fails, it becomes the opponent's turn to announce a number of questions from one through three, and their formats and chapters.

3. If a player uses up the last question(s) in any chapter, the opponent may complete the round by answering questions of the same format from any of the chapters 2, 9, 10, or 11.

4. The first player to get three strikes loses.

Quick Reference Chart

	Number of Players	Solitaire Version?	Question Chapters Used
Game One: First to Finish	2-4	Yes	2
Game Two: Boxing	2-3	Yes	3-8
Game Three: Checkout	2-6	No	3-8
Game Four: Twenty-One	2-6	No	9-11
Game Five: Challenge Trivia	2*	No	9-11
Game Six: Double or Nothing	2-4	Yes	9-11
Game Seven: Strikeout	2*	No	2-12

*Or 2 teams

Chapter 2

Question Sets

Answers to questions in this chapter begin on page 167.

Question Set 1

True or False?

(1-Point Questions)

2.1 The Eiffel Tower is taller than the Washington Monument. [36]

2.2 Some fish do not lay eggs, but instead give birth to live young. [122]

2.3 Among 20th century British prime ministers, Margaret Thatcher has served the longest. [201]

2.4 No Academy Award for best actor or best actress has ever been given to a performer in his or her first movie. [72]

2.5 According to Emily Post, it is improper to use both a fork and spoon to eat pie à la mode. [196]

2.6 United States senators have a higher salary than members of the House of Representatives. [51]

2.7 No character referred to by name in the title of any play by William Shakespeare is alive at the end of the play. [106]

2.8 In Ernest Thayer's poem "Casey at the Bat," "mighty Casey" hits a game-winning home run in the bottom of the ninth inning. [182]

Multiple Choice

(2-Point Questions)

2.9 The largest McDonald's in the world opened in January, 1990, with 700 seats and 27 cash registers. Where is it? [188]
   A. London
   B. Moscow
   C. Tokyo

2.10 The increase in the cost of a first-class postage stamp (to 30 cents) due to happen in early 1991 was not unusual. How many times did the U.S. Post Office raise the cost of a first-class stamp between 1960 and 1990? [93]
   A. 3
   B. 7
   C. 10

2.11 When Clint Eastwood appeared in the classic "spaghetti western" *The Good, the Bad, and the Ugly*, what role did he play? [160]
   A. the Good
   B. the Bad
   C. the Ugly

2.12 If all the gold ever mined were squeezed into a single cube, about how long would one edge of the cube be? [128]
  A. 56 feet
  B. 560 feet
  C. 5,600 feet

2.13 For what kind of music have L.L. Cool J, Salt & Pepa, and Kool Moe Dee been nominated for Grammy Awards? [3]
  A. rap
  B. rock
  C. soul

2.14 Who was the first to win two consecutive Academy Awards for best actor? [225]
  A. Marlon Brando
  B. James Stewart
  C. Spencer Tracy

2.15 What fraction of the delegates to the 1988 Democratic Convention had been delegates to a previous convention? [81]
  A. fewer than one half
  B. more than one half but fewer than three quarters
  C. more than three quarters

2.16 What is the British name for the pencil-and-paper game known in the U.S. as "tic-tac-toe"? [115]
  A. niminy-piminy
  B. noughts and crosses
  C. three bobbies

(3-Point Questions)

2.17 Who was the first divorced person to be president of the United States? [204]
  A. Thomas Jefferson
  B. Franklin Delano Roosevelt
  C. Gerald Ford
  D. Ronald Reagan

2.18 What are Asahi, Kirin, Sapporo, and Suntory? [19]
   A. four Japanese car makers
   B. four brands of Japanese beer
   C. four dangerous creatures of Japanese mythology
   D. four styles of Japanese art

2.19 In approximate terms, how did the size of the U.S.
   national debt change from 1980 to 1990? [175]
   A. It decreased from $2 trillion to $1 trillion.
   B. It increased from $500 billion to $1 trillion.
   C. It increased from $1 trillion to $3 trillion.
   D. It increased from $2 trillion to $3 trillion.

2.20 What is Africa's most populous country? [59]
   A. Egypt
   B. Ethiopia
   C. Nigeria
   D. South Africa

2.21 According to AT&T, on what day are the most
   long-distance phone calls placed? [197]
   A. Christmas
   B. Father's Day
   C. Mother's Day
   D. Thanksgiving

2.22 In what year did Roger Bannister become the first person
   ever to run a mile in less than four minutes? [99]
   A. 1914
   B. 1934
   C. 1954
   D. 1974

2.23 As of 1990, what movie had grossed more money at the
   box office than any other movie in history? [236]
   A. *Batman*
   B. *E.T.*
   C. *Gone With the Wind*
   D. *Star Wars*

2.24 As of 1991, how many teams does California have, in total, in baseball's two major leagues, the National Football League, and the National Basketball Association? [138]
A. 7
B. 9
C. 11
D. 13

2.25 In Lewis Carroll's nonsense poem "Jabberwocky," all but which of the following creatures are mentioned? [40]
A. bandersnatch
B. jabberwock
C. jubjub bird
D. snark

Question Set 2

True or False?

(1-Point Questions)

2.26 Rolls Royce Motor Cars, Ltd. makes Bentleys as well as Rolls Royces. [209]

2.27 The course for a marathon race is exactly 26 miles long. [22]

2.28 Elvis Presley had over 100 records that made *Billboard's* Top 40. [114]

2.29 Regulations allow postal workers to carry firearms to protect themselves from robbers and hostile dogs. [176]

2.30 In the National Hockey League Entry Drafts, no hockey player born in the United States has ever been chosen in the first round. [45]

2.31 Blue whales, alive today, weigh more (out of water) than the largest dinosaurs. [226]

2.32 Camp David, the presidential retreat, was named after David Eisenhower. [87]

2.33 The lines "I am the master of my fate;/I am the captain of my soul" are from a poem by Henry Wadsworth Longfellow. [198]

Multiple Choice

(2-Point Questions)

2.34 What company was forced out of India in 1977 for refusing to disclose its secret formula? [123]
   A. Coca Cola
   B. Dr. Pepper
   C. YooHoo

2.35 A $20 gold piece set a record in May, 1989 for the highest amount ever paid for an American coin. How much? [58]
   A. $135,000
   B. $1,350,000
   C. $13,500,000

2.36 According to legend, the king of what mythical, long-sought kingdom is covered once a year with oil and gold dust, becoming "the Golden One"? [154]
   A. Amazonia
   B. El Dorado
   C. Shangri-La

2.37 What is the name of the masked killer in the *Friday the 13th* movies? [244]
   A. Freddy
   B. Jason
   C. He has no name.

2.38 How long after being launched did it take *Voyager 2* to reach Neptune? [33]
   A. 6 months
   B. 3 years
   C. 12 years

2.39 Maine is the only state in the U.S. that borders exactly one other state. What is the state it borders? [10]
   A. Massachusetts
   B. New Hampshire
   C. Vermont

2.40 In major league baseball, which of these baseball players set a record for having the lowest batting average while leading his league in home runs? [67]
   A. Reggie Jackson
   B. Dave Kingman
   C. Darryl Strawberry

2.41 Whose debut album titled *Forever Your Girl* sold over 5 million records? [205]
   A. Paula Abdul
   B. Sade
   C. Tiffany

(3-Point Questions)

2.42 Approximately what percentage of American households consist of a working father, a housewife mother, and children under the age of 18? [139]
   A. 10 percent
   B. 30 percent
   C. 50 percent
   D. 70 percent

2.43 According to the *Playboy Bar Guide*, which of these is *not* used in a Bloody Mary? [177]
   A. ketchup
   B. sugar
   C. tabasco sauce
   D. Worcestershire sauce

2.44 What state is known as the Badger State? [50]
  A. Michigan
  B. Minnesota
  C. Oregon
  D. Wisconsin

2.45 In a 1988 production of Neil Simon's *The Odd Couple* at a Dallas dinner theater, what former Dallas Cowboy football star played sportswriter Oscar Madison? [229]
  A. Ed "Too Tall" Jones
  B. Harvey Martin
  C. Don Meredith
  D. Roger Staubach

2.46 From what company did United Telecommunications buy much of Sprint, the long distance telephone company? [103]
  A. AT&T
  B. General Electric
  C. GTE Corporation
  D. IBM

2.47 The Pulitzer committee erred by awarding its 1950 drama prize only to Richard Rodgers and Oscar Hammerstein II. Later, the committee added the name of Joshua Logan, who had coauthored and directed the play. What was the play? [192]
  A. *Carousel*
  B. *Mister Roberts*
  C. *Oklahoma*
  D. *South Pacific*

2.48 Who holds the National League record for hitting the most home runs in a single season? [6]
  A. Hank Aaron
  B. Ralph Kiner
  C. Willie Mays
  D. Hack Wilson

2.49 Who wrote the narrative poem *Eugene Onegin*, which was made into a ballet by John Cranko? [82]
  A. Jacques Brel
  B. Lord Byron
  C. Archibald MacLeish
  D. Alexander Pushkin

2.50 Approximately how much vegetable oil is produced each year worldwide? [242]
  A. 40 million ounces
  B. 40 million pounds
  C. 40 million kilograms
  D. 40 million tons

Question Set 3

True or False?

(I-Point Questions)

2.51 The movie *Star Wars* takes place in the 27th Century A.D. [94]

2.52 When pitcher Tommy John made three errors in one inning in a 1988 baseball game, he tied the major league record for most errors in an inning by a single player. [29]

2.53 In area, the state of Alaska is more than twice as large as Texas. [61]

2.54 Each winter, squirrels lose about half their nuts because they forget where they stored them. [231]

2.55 The first Roman emperor was Julius Caesar. [134]

2.56 In Greek mythology, Pegasus was a white horse with wings. [174]

2.57 The English language version of the Christmas carol "Adeste Fidelis" is "O Come All Ye Faithful." [16]

2.58 Two of the greatest artists of all time, Leonardo da Vinci and Michelangelo Buonarroti, were both alive in the year 1500. [38]

Multiple Choice

(2-Point Questions)

2.59 What American's 1987 tour of the Soviet Union was the subject of a documentary called *A Matter of Trust*? [219]
  A. Jane Fonda
  B. Billy Graham
  C. Billy Joel

2.60 The legendary Archer William Tell was of what nationality? [110]
  A. Austrian
  B. German
  C. Swiss

2.61 What was the last film in which John Wayne appeared? [199]
  A. *The Green Berets*
  B. *The Shootist*
  C. *True Grit*

2.62 Which planet takes only about 10 Earth hours to rotate once on its axis? [147]
  A. Mars
  B. Mercury
  C. Jupiter

2.63 Where was Lincoln born? [77]
  A. Illinois
  B. Indiana
  C. Kentucky

2.64 What Cincinnati Reds star was the only player to win two consecutive Most Valuable Player awards in the 1970s? [233]
A. Johnny Bench
B. Joe Morgan
C. Pete Rose

2.65 On the TV sitcom *Roseanne*, what is Roseanne's last name? [118]
A. Connor
B. Denton
C. Richards

2.66 Under terms of collective bargaining agreements, which major sport pays the highest minimum salary? [144]
A. baseball
B. basketball
C. football

(3-Point Questions)

2.67 What is pictured on the back of a $10 bill? [191]
A. the Capitol building
B. the signing of the Declaration of Independence
C. the Treasury building
D. the White House

2.68 In which book of the Old Testament does the Lord appear to Moses in the form of a burning bush? [46]
A. *Genesis*
B. *Exodus*
C. *Numbers*
D. *Deuteronomy*

2.69 What toy company makes Barbie dolls? [243]
A. Hasbro
B. Lewis Galoob Toys
C. Mattel
D. Milton Bradley

2.70 In which of these presidential elections would the outcome have been unchanged if presidents were elected by popular vote rather than by the electoral college system? [129]
   A. in 1824, when John Quincy Adams defeated Andrew Jackson
   B. in 1828, when Andrew Jackson defeated John Quincy Adams
   C. in 1876, when Rutherford B. Hayes defeated Samuel Tilden
   D. in 1888, when Benjamin Harrison defeated Grover Cleveland

2.71 As of 1990, who held the major league record for the most stolen bases in one season? [186]
   A. Lou Brock
   B. Ricky Henderson
   C. Willie Mays
   D. Maury Wills

2.72 Who was not one of *The Three Musketeers*? [66]
   A. Aramis
   B. Athos
   C. D'Artagnan
   D. Porthos

2.73 In the National Football League, each team has 11 players on the field at any given time. How many did each team have in the short-lived, late '80s indoor sport of Arena football? [153]
   A. 5
   B. 8
   C. 11
   D. 14

2.74 Francis Ford Coppola put up some of his own money to finish *Apocalypse Now* when it ran wildly over budget. Of the $30 million the film eventually cost, how much did he put up himself? [171]
   A. $1 million
   B. $6 million
   C. $16 million
   D. $25 million

2.75 In 1989, what play by Wendy Wasserstein won both a
     Pulitzer Prize for drama and a Tony Award for best play?
     [24]
     A. *Breathing Lessons*
     B. *Into the Woods*
     C. *Rumors*
     D. *The Heidi Chronicles*

Question Set 4

True or False?

(1-Point Questions)

2.76 The term "Fleet Street" refers to the British financial
     establishment. [9]

2.77 Actor Tom Selleck was a real-life navy commander. [121]

2.78 Giuseppe Verdi died at the age of 37 without ever seeing
     his opera *La Traviata* performed on stage. [30]

2.79 The World Cup soccer championships, the Indianapolis
     500 auto race, and the Tour de France bicycle race all
     originated in the 20th century. [149]

2.80 Each player in a backgammon game begins with 12
     pieces. [88]

2.81 Wild marsupials, which include kangaroos and many
     other pouched mammals, live only in the Southern
     Hemisphere. [214]

2.82 "Poltergeist" literally means "noisy ghost." [57]

2.83 In 1911, British explorers became the first to reach the
     South Pole. [194]

Multiple Choice

(2-Point Questions)

2.84 Blondie's number one hit single "Call Me" was the theme
song of what motion picture? [140]
  A. *American Gigolo*
  B. *An Officer and a Gentleman*
  C. *Sorry, Wrong Number*

2.85 In 1985, 5 percent of U.S. households had telephone
answering machines. How many had them by 1990? [14]
  A. 11 percent
  B. 31 percent
  C. 51 percent

2.86 What country of 3 million persons, a few years ago,
routinely required foreign visitors to wade through a
trough of disinfectant as they entered the country? [220]
  A. Albania
  B. Cuba
  C. Mongolia

2.87 Who wrote the song containing the line "Mad dogs and
Englishmen go out in the mid-day sun"? [60]
  A. Noel Coward
  B. Gilbert and Sullivan
  C. Cole Porter

2.88 When it is noon in Los Angeles, California, what time is
it in Honolulu, Hawaii, assuming both cities are on
standard time? [150]
  A. 8 a.m.
  B. 10 a.m.
  C. 2 p.m.

2.89 The Blair House at 1651 Pennsylvania Avenue in
Washington, D.C. is the nation's guest house. For whom
is it named? [41]
  A. a Confederate Civil War general
  B. the first surgeon-general of the Army
  C. the founder of *The Globe* newspaper

2.90 During the decade of the 1980s, what major league team spent the most money on player salaries? [217]
A. California Angels
B. Los Angeles Dodgers
C. New York Yankees

2.91 About how much does a cubic foot of water weigh? [27]
A. 10.0 pounds
B. 37.2 pounds
C. 62.4 pounds

(3 Point Questions)

2.92 What U.S. city, which celebrated its bicentennial in 1988, is known as the Queen City? [232]
A. Atlanta
B. Cincinnati
C. Louisville
D. Memphis

2.93 "Sweet potato" is a nickname for what musical instrument? [108]
A. accordion
B. bagpipes
C. ocarina
D. pipe organ

2.94 The Baby Ruth candy bar was named not for Babe Ruth but, according to most reports, for a U.S. president's daughter Ruth, who would often play on the front lawn of the White House. Who was Ruth's father? [74]
A. Grover Cleveland
B. Calvin Coolidge
C. Herbert Hoover
D. William Howard Taft

2.95 Which of these colors is *not* used for an official karate belt? [210]
A. blue
B. purple
C. white
D. yellow

2.96 Cy Young had the most career victories of any major
league pitcher. Who had the second most victories? [31]
A. Grover Cleveland Alexander
B. Walter Johnson
C. Christy Mathewson
D. Warren Spahn

2.97 In which card game do players keep score with a
pegboard? [248]
A. cribbage
B. euchre
C. hearts
D. whist

2.98 How many sides does a dodecagon have? [137]
A. 10
B. 12
C. 15
D. 20

2.99 In fiction, where can Gillikin Country, Munchkin
Country, Quadling Country, and Winkie Country all be
found? [83]
A. the Land of Oz
B. Middle Earth
C. Never-Never Land
D. Transylvania

2.100 Who wrote the musical work *The Sorcerer's Apprentice*?
[179]
A. Paul Dukas
B. Wolfgang Amadeus Mozart
C. Maurice Ravel
D. Camille Saint-Saens

Question Set 5

True or False?

(1-Point Questions)

2.101 In tennis, a player who throws the racket at the ball automatically loses the point. [69]

2.102 Water, unlike most other compounds, expands when it freezes. [105]

2.103 The U.S. Navy's unofficial motto "Don't give up the ship!" was taken from an exhortation by John Paul Jones. [159]

2.104 Wine sales steadily increased in the U.S. from 1987 through 1990. [238]

2.105 In 1988, Jose Canseco became the first major league baseball player ever to have both 40 or more home runs and 40 or more stolen bases in a single season. [95]

2.106 The last state to enter the United States was Alaska. [1]

2.107 In the winter of 1987-88, the rock star Prince recorded an entire album titled *The Black Album*, but then decided not to release it. [203]

2.108 *Dallas* was the first prime-time soap opera on U.S. television. [21]

Multiple Choice

(2-Point Questions)

2.109 Based on 1989 sales, what percentage of all the beer in
the U.S. is made by Anheuser-Busch? [101]
A. 22%
B. 42%
C. 62%

2.110 Who was the first NFL player to be selected to the Pro
Bowl nine times in his first nine seasons in the league?
[155]
A. Jim Brown
B. Jack Lambert
C. Lawrence Taylor

2.111 In the late 1950s, what former silent film actress played
Esmerelda Nugent on *The Gale Storm Show*? [249]
A. Ethel Barrymore
B. Fay Holden
C. Zazu Pitts

2.112 What is the best approximation of the U.S. population as
of 1990? [78]
A. 225 million
B. 250 million
C. 275 million

2.113 Who won nine New York City marathons during the
1980s? [135]
A. Joan Benoit
B. Alberto Salazar
C. Grete Waitz

2.114 "The Gift of the Magi" and other short stories of
O'Henry are famous for what? [169]
A. religious subjects
B. sexual explicitness
C. surprise endings

2.115 What is the name of the award that goes to the best collegiate golfer of the year? [47]
  A. the Nelson Trophy
  B. the Nicklaus Award
  C. the Ryder Cup

2.116 Diana Vreeland was a magazine editor and consultant in what field? [187]
  A. fashion
  B. food
  C. interior design

(3-Point Questions)

2.117 In 1987 and 1988, 600,000 Mozambique refugees went to what neighboring country, giving that country the highest ratio of refugees to local population of any country in the world? [124]
  A. Malawi
  B. South Africa
  C. Sudan
  D. Tanzania

2.118 Ernö Rubik, a professor of architecture and design at the Academy of Arts and Crafts in Budapest, Hungary, has lent his name to three different puzzle products. Which of the following is *not* one of them? [200]
  A. Rubik's Clock
  B. Rubik's Cube
  C. Rubik's Magic
  D. Rubik's World

2.119 When the current tennis ranking system began in 1973, what male tennis pro was ranked number one? [65]
  A. Bjorn Borg
  B. Jimmy Connors
  C. Ilie Nastase
  D. John Newcombe

2.120 In the series of movies starring Clint Eastwood as "Dirty Harry," what is Harry's last name? [247]
A. Callahan
B. Flint
C. Harrigan
D. Steele

2.121 "MI" is the official postal abbreviation for which state? [152]
A. Michigan
B. Minnesota
C. Mississippi
D. Missouri

2.122 The dog mentioned in Vice President Richard Nixon's "Checkers" speech was what breed? [211]
A. beagle
B. cocker spaniel
C. Dalmatian
D. Scottie

2.123 Who wrote "Rip Van Winkle"? [90]
A. James Fenimore Cooper
B. Nathaniel Hawthorne
C. Washington Irving
D. Robert Louis Stevenson

2.124 Which of these dishes is not typically made with some kind of seafood? [250]
A. bouillabaisse
B. osso buco
C. fritto misto
D. tempura

2.125 Who once said publicly, "Sometimes you have to go above the written law"? [5]
A. Al Capone
B. G. Gordon Liddy
C. Fawn Hall
D. Jimmy Swaggart

Question Set 6

True or False?

(1-Point Questions)

2.126 The Lincoln head penny, counting all its design variations, is the most numerous U.S. coin ever minted. [17]

2.127 Greece is the world's leading producer of olives. [222]

2.128 Through 1990, there has never been a year in which a foreign car was the best-selling passenger car in the U.S. [76]

2.129 Track stars Jackie Joyner-Kersee and Florence Griffith Joyner are sisters-in-law. [43]

2.130 Bulls are more likely to attack when they see red. [127]

2.131 Lincoln's Emancipation Proclamation freed all the slaves in both the Northern and Southern states. [163]

2.132 The first stadium built especially for football was at Harvard. [100]

2.133 The paintings stolen from Boston's Isabella Stewart Gardner Museum in March 1990 (the largest art theft in history) were not insured. [2]

Multiple Choice

(2-Point Questions)

2.134 A group of lions is called a "pride." What word describes a group of cows? [185]
A. a barn
B. a colony
C. a murder

2.135 What foreign country has the most money invested in the U.S.? [54]
A. Canada
B. Japan
C. United Kingdom

2.136 Which novel by John Steinbeck is about Tom Joad and his family of migrant farm workers? [111]
A. *Cannery Row*
B. *The Grapes of Wrath*
C. *Of Mice and Men*

2.137 When it was founded in 1945, the United Nations had 51 members. How many members does it have today? [28]
A. 59
B. 109
C. 159

2.138 Which of these cities is the capital of Iowa? [145]
A. Cedar Rapids
B. Davenport
C. Des Moines

2.139 From 1980 to 1990, what state had the highest percentage increase in population? [246]
A. Alaska
B. Arizona
C. Florida

2.140 In 1988, for the first time, the same university won both the men's and women's National Collegiate All-Sports title, which combines the rankings of the schools in a wide variety of sports. What was this top athletic school? [91]
A. Oklahoma
B. Texas
C. UCLA

2.141 What comedian and member of the Kay Kyser troupe, known for such nonsense songs as "Three Little Fishies," was a regular on the 1949-50 quiz show *Kay Kyser's Kollege of Musical Knowledge*? [37]
A. Steve Allen
B. Jimmy Durante
C. Ish Kabibble

(3-Point Questions)

2.142 This "Father of the Constitution" was also the only U.S. president to actively lead troops while in office. Who was he? [206]
A. George Washington
B. Thomas Jefferson
C. James Madison
D. Andrew Jackson

2.143 In the National Hockey League, which of these is *not* the name of a division? [119]
A. Adams
B. Norris
C. Smythe
D. Wales

2.144 Three of these movie sequels were released in 1988. Which one was released earlier? [240]
A. *Arthur 2: On the Rocks*
B. *Caddyshack II*
C. *Crocodile Dundee II*
D. *Poltergeist II*

2.145 Who wrote the sonnet that begins, "Much have I travell'd in the realms of gold"? [15]
    A. John Donne
    B. John Keats
    C. John Milton
    D. John Smith

2.146 What is a fandango? [218]
    A. a dance
    B. a food
    C. a grass skirt
    D. a hat

2.147 Who was the first black American pictured on a U.S. postage stamp? [102]
    A. Louis Armstrong
    B. Frederick Douglass
    C. Joe Louis
    D. Booker T. Washington

2.148 In Aussie slang, a "bluey" is someone who: [161]
    A. deals in pornography.
    B. has reddish hair.
    C. is sad.
    D. wears very little in cold weather.

2.149 Who wrote the piano piece known as "The Minute Waltz"? [130]
    A. Johannes Brahms
    B. Frédéric Chopin
    C. Franz Liszt
    D. Sergei Rachmaninoff

2.150 Whose real name was Thomas Lanier Williams? [184]
    A. Andy Williams
    B. Robin Williams
    C. Ted Williams
    D. Tennessee Williams

Question Set 7

True or False?

(1-Point Questions)

2.151 In lunch-counter slang, a "CB" means "coffee, black."
[89]

2.152 Sara Gilbert of the TV comedy *Roseanne* is the younger
sister of actress Melissa Gilbert. [8]

2.153 One furlong is equal to a tenth of a mile. [223]

2.154 Except for teams from New York and California, no
World Series has ever been played between teams from
the same state. [49]

2.155 The Central Time Zone includes all or part of more states
than any other U.S. time zone. [172]

2.156 The berries of the poison ivy plant are yellowish-white in
color. [34]

2.157 Amelia Earhart was the first woman to receive the
Distinguished Flying Cross. [213]

2.158 "It's Too Late" is the only *Billboard* number one single
Carole King has ever recorded. [85]

Multiple Choice

(2-Point Questions)

2.159 What is the name of Donald Regan's controversial book
recalling his days as Ronald Reagan's Treasury Secretary
and Chief of Staff? [141]
A. *Astrology, Anyone?*
B. *For the Record*
C. *Off the Record*

2.160 What is Myanmar the name of? [234]
A. the country that was formerly called Burma
B. a moon of Neptune discovered in 1989
C. a new kind of "stick-together" fabric, similar to
Velcro

2.161 In the opera *Faust*, Faust wins Marguerite's love with a
box full of what? [71]
A. candy
B. jewelry
C. roses

2.162 In music, which of the following are "accidentals"? [183]
A. finger cymbals and castanets
B. mistakes made while playing
C. sharps and flats

2.163 The keynote speaker at the 1988 Democratic Convention
was Ann Richards. What office did she hold at the time?
[131]
A. governor of Kentucky
B. state treasurer of Texas
C. U.S. senator from Missouri

2.164 At an international gathering of scientists in Moscow in
1988, Leonid Gorshkov of the main Soviet space agency
told the group that it was "inevitable" that humans would
land on Mars by what year? [12]
A. 2000
B. 2010
C. 2040

2.165 In 1989, the Big Ten conference decided to admit what additional, eleventh school? [227]
A. Cincinnati
B. Notre Dame
C. Penn State

2.166 In 1951, the U.S. Constitution and Declaration of Independence were sealed in protective glass cases filled with what gas? [64]
A. carbon dioxide
B. helium
C. nitrogen

(3-Point Questions)

2.167 What city did Jack the Ripper terrorize in the 19th century? [245]
A. Belfast
B. London
C. New York
D. San Francisco

2.168 In 1990, the average major league baseball player's salary was about how many times more than the average player's salary was in 1970? [98]
A. 2 times more
B. 5 times more
C. 10 times more
D. 20 times more

2.169 Which comic opera by Gilbert and Sullivan contains the songs "A wandering minstrel I" and "Titwillow"? [173]
A. *The Gondoliers*
B. *The Mikado*
C. *H.M.S. Pinafore*
D. *The Pirates of Penzance*

2.170 What men's college basketball team, nicknamed the
"Blue Devils," reached the Final Four of the N.C.A.A.
tournament four times in five years, from 1986 through
1990? [42]
A. Duke
B. Georgetown
C. Nevada-Las Vegas
D. Villanova

2.171 More than 75% of Botswana's total revenue comes from
what industry? [235]
A. cattle
B. coffee
C. diamonds
D. tourism

2.172 According to *The Book of Jargon*, to what does the term
"tranny" refer? [56]
A. a car's "gearbox"
B. a man who wears women's clothes
C. a person's preferred style of meditation
D. an urban transportation system

2.173 Who wrote the sonnet that begins, "The world is charged
with the grandeur of God"? [158]
A. Gerard Manley Hopkins
B. Henry Wadsworth Longfellow
C. Alfred, Lord Tennyson
D. Oscar Wilde

2.174 What are you if you're "non compos mentis"? [193]
A. financially destitute
B. mentally unstable
C. physically repulsive
D. pregnant

2.175 Which of these persons lived to see his or her 50th
birthday? [23]
A. Enrico Caruso
B. Davy Crockett
C. Edith Piaf
D. William Shakespeare

Question Set 8

True or False?

(1-point Questions)

2.176 The movie *The China Syndrome* was loosely based on the nuclear accident at Three Mile Island. [7]

2.177 The distress signal "SOS" stands for "Save Our Souls." [62]

2.178 No racehorse won the Triple Crown during the 1980s. [133]

2.179 Your nose stops growing when you reach the age of 20 or so. [208]

2.180 The Boston Tea Party took place about one month after the Declaration of Independence was signed. [53]

2.181 The group The Four Seasons was formed in Newark, New Jersey, under the name "The Four Lovers." [228]

2.182 Lawyers take the Hippocratic oath before entering their profession. [113]

2.183 The six *Brandenburg Concertos* are by Georg Friedrich Handel. [178]

Multiple Choice

(2-Point Questions)

2.184 As in the comic strip *The Katzenjammer Kids*, what does the German word "Katzenjammer" mean? [20]
  A. bicycle pump
  B. hangover
  C. mischievous

2.185 Packages sent via Federal Express are routinely routed through the company's headquarters in what city? [216]
   A. Chicago
   B. Kansas City
   C. Memphis

2.186 In 1980, Tom Weiskopf tied an undesirable record for the most strokes taken on a single hole in the Masters golf tournament. How many strokes? [109]
   A. 7
   B. 10
   C. 13

2.187 Who played the title role in the 1946 film *The She-Wolf of London*? [195]
   A. Eva Gabor
   B. Boris Karloff
   C. June Lockhart

2.188 What two countries border the Dead Sea? [97]
   A. Israel and Egypt
   B. Israel and Jordan
   C. Jordan and Saudi Arabia

2.189 What form of poker is played at the annual World Series of Poker in Las Vegas? [162]
   A. five card stud
   B. five card draw
   C. hold 'em

2.190 Since World War II, the Army-Navy football game has usually been played in what city? [125]
   A. Chicago
   B. Philadelphia
   C. West Point

2.191 At the end of the opera *Don Giovanni*, what does Don Giovanni descend into? [237]
   A. hell
   B. insanity
   C. prison

(3-Point Questions)

2.192 Carlos Salinas de Gortari of the ruling Institutional Revolutionary Party won a controversial 1988 presidential election in which his opponents made accusations of voting fraud. What is his country? [35]
A. El Salvador
B. Mexico
C. Nicaragua
D. Spain

2.193 Who set an all-time career record by hitting six home runs in All-Star baseball games? [156]
A. Hank Aaron
B. Johnny Bench
C. Willie Mays
D. Stan Musial

2.194 What is the main alcoholic ingredient in a zombie? [207]
A. beer
B. brandy
C. rum
D. whiskey

2.195 What does a gangster call his "mouthpiece"? [79]
A. his bodyguard
B. his girlfriend
C. his gun
D. his lawyer

2.196 According to the Bible, who designed Noah's Ark? [221]
A. God
B. Noah
C. Noah's son
D. Noah's wife

2.197 Whom did Bobby Fischer defeat in the 1972 chess tournament held in Reykjavik, Iceland? [117]
A. Tigran Petrosian
B. Anatoly Karpov
C. Gary Kasparov
D. Boris Spassky

2.198 Which cruise line operates the *Queen Elizabeth II*? [241]
    A. Carnival
    B. Cunard
    C. Grace

2.199 In Norton Juster's 1962 novel *The Phantom Tollbooth*, the city of Dictionopolis is the rival of what other city? [84]
    A. Alphaville
    B. Audiopolis
    C. Digitopolis
    D. Metropolis

2.200 What is the main ingredient in the manufacture of pewter? [146]
    A. copper
    B. iron
    C. lead
    D. tin

Question Set 9

True or False?

(1-Point Questions)

2.201 In the United States Army, a lieutenant general outranks a major general. [164]

2.202 Nadia Comaneci of Romania and Mary Lou Retton of the United States were helped to Olympic championships by the same coach. [26]

2.203 The sequel to the movie *The Guns of Navarone* was titled *Navarone Sunday*. [224]

2.204 Adult koala bears are notorious milk-drinkers. [96]

2.205 Joan of Arc died on a battlefield in France. [132]

2.206 Due at least in part to the amount of revenue taken in by casinos in Monte Carlo, residents of Monaco pay no income tax. [180]

2.207 *The Diary of Samuel Pepys* was actually written by Charles Dickens. [63]

2.208 The most common first name in the world is "John." [86]

Multiple Choice

(2-Point Questions)

2.209 Because of a verdict for $10.3 billion in favor of Pennzoil, what major oil company spent a year in bankruptcy? [166]
   A. Exxon
   B. Mobil
   C. Texaco

2.210 To stamp collectors, what are "cinderellas"? [116]
   A. stamps issued privately, such as Christmas seals
   B. stamps that look unattractive but have a high value
   C. stamps that look attractive but have a low value

2.211 Frank Sinatra, Bruce Springsteen, and Paul Simon were all born in what state? [189]
   A. California
   B. New Jersey
   C. New York

2.212 On TV's *Wheel of Fortune*, how much does it cost to "buy a vowel"? [44]
   A. $150
   B. $200
   C. $250

2.213 What kind of poem is Edward Lear famous for? [239]
   A. ballad
   B. limerick
   C. sonnet

2.214 In the 1960s, a group of businessmen bought London
   Bridge for $2.5 million and moved it where? [143]
   A. Lake Havasu City, Arizona
   B. Peoria, Illinois
   C. Truth or Consequences, New Mexico

2.215 In 1990, Jim Palmer was elected to the Hall of Fame with
   the second-highest vote percentage ever for a pitcher.
   What pitcher had the highest vote total? [70]
   A. Bob Feller
   B. Bob Gibson
   C. Sandy Koufax

2.216 What two countries together have over 90 percent of the
   world's reserves of platinum? [215]
   A. Australia and South Africa
   B. Canada and the United States
   C. South Africa and the Soviet Union

(3-Point Questions)

2.217 The United States has only had one vice president who
   was born in California. Who was it? [55]
   A. Gerald Ford
   B. Richard Nixon
   C. Harry Truman
   D. Henry Wallace

2.218 What major league player is third, behind Hank Aaron
   and Babe Ruth, in career home runs? [151]
   A. Reggie Jackson
   B. Harmon Killebrew
   C. Willie Mays
   D. Frank Robinson

2.219 Who wrote the lines, "Oh, East is East, and West is West, /
And never the twain shall meet"? [181]
A. Lord Byron
B. G.K. Chesterton
C. Thomas Hood
D. Rudyard Kipling

2.220 Who starred as Sally Bowles in the original Broadway
production of *Cabaret*? [112]
A. Julie Andrews
B. Carol Channing
C. Jill Haworth
D. Liza Minnelli

2.221 What company went into Chapter 11 bankruptcy in 1988,
despite selling the very popular Cabbage Patch Kids doll
and Trivial Pursuit game at that time? [136]
A. Coleco
B. Ideal
C. Selchow & Righter
D. Worlds of Wonder

2.222 As measured in monetary value, Canada buys about one
fifth of all United States exports. Approximately what
fraction of Canadian exports does the United States buy?
[168]
A. one tenth
B. one fifth
C. one half
D. three quarters

2.223 According to a late 1980s survey of 40,000 students,
done by the National Institute of Dental Research,
approximately what fraction of American school children
now have no decay in their permanent teeth? [25]
A. one tenth
B. one quarter
C. one third
D. one half

2.224 According to the *Random House Dictionary*, which of the following is "the Holy Land"? [230]
   A. Israel
   B. Lebanon
   C. Palestine
   D. Syria

2.225 What country produces the most potatoes? [4]
   A. China
   B. Ireland
   C. Soviet Union
   D. United States

Question Set 10

True or False?

(1-Point Questions)

2.226 Jefferson Davis, president of the Confederacy during the Civil War, was previously the United States Secretary of War. [39]

2.227 Size "A" batteries are larger than size "D" batteries. [73]

2.228 "The mass of men lead lives of quiet desperation" was written by Henry David Thoreau. [104]

2.229 On the sixth day, if the Old Testament account is accurate, God created wombats. [167]

2.230 Bette Midler's "Wind Beneath My Wings," which won a Grammy Award as record of the year for 1989, was her first number one hit. [13]

2.231 The name of the Wimbledon tennis trophy is the Challenge Cup. [126]

2.232 Kangaroo rats can be found in the United States, while rat kangaroos can be found in Australia. [148]

2.233 The line "All animals are equal, but some animals are more equal than others" is from A.A. Milne's *The House on Pooh Corner*. [52]

Multiple Choice

(2-Point Questions)

2.234 What is the traditional gift for a 40th wedding anniversary? [80]
A. diamond
B. emerald
C. ruby

2.235 What is the main ingredient in vichyssoise? [212]
A. clams
B. lima beans
C. potatoes
D. tomatoes

2.236 Akitas, briards, and samoyeds are kinds of what? [142]
A. cats
B. dogs
C. flowers

2.237 From 1985 to 1990, how much did the percentage of U.S. households owning VCRs increase? [32]
A. It doubled.
B. It tripled.
C. It quadrupled.

2.238 *Far From the Madding Crowd* and *Tess of the d'Urbervilles* are among the novels of which author? [190]
A. Truman Capote
B. Thomas Hardy
C. John Steinbeck

2.239 At the end of the opera *Tosca*, what does Tosca throw
from the roof of the prison? [11]
   A. her handkerchief
   B. her roses
   C. herself

2.240 Bell Tower, Orobelle, and Jupiter are varieties of what
vegetable? [68]
   A. onion
   B. pepper
   C. squash

2.241 The quotation, "With malice toward none; with charity
for all" is from what speech by Abraham Lincoln? [157]
   A. First Inaugural Address
   B. Gettysburg Address
   C. Second Inaugural Address

(3-Point Questions)

2.242 In a quarter-mile race, which animal can generally outrun
the other three? [92]
   A. giraffe
   B. lion
   C. pronghorn antelope
   D. quarter horse

2.243 Which of the following songs is *not* from the musical
Fiddler on the Roof? [170]
   A. "Do You Love Me?"
   B. "Shalom"
   C. "To Life"
   D. "Sunrise, Sunset"

2.244 While he was mayor of Buffalo, New York, he was named the Beast of Buffalo; but later, this U.S. president was also known by such nicknames as the Perpetual Candidate, His Obstinancy, and the Sage of Princeton. Who was he? [48]
A. Grover Cleveland
B. Millard Fillmore
C. Franklin Delano Roosevelt
D. Theodore Roosevelt

2.245 Which of these actors did *not* star in the 1989 film *Family Business*? [107]
A. Matthew Broderick
B. Sean Connery
C. Tom Cruise
D. Dustin Hoffman

2.246 In 1988, after reaching agreement with Melanesian separatists, France announced that it would hold a referendum on self-determination in what overseas territory in 1998? [202]
A. French Guiana
B. Guadeloupe
C. Martinique
D. New Caledonia

2.247 Actor Paul Newman has ventured into the business of selling all but which one of the following foods? [75]
A. cookies
B. popcorn
C. salad dressing
D. spaghetti sauce

2.248 Approximately how many beverage cans are made in the U.S. annually? [120]
A. 800 million
B. 8 billion
C. 80 billion
D. 800 billion

2.249 Which of these is *not* the title of a novel by James A. Michener? [165]
  A. *Alaska*
  B. *Hawaii*
  C. *Poland*
  D. *Russia*

2.250 For six consecutive years during the 1980s, what breed of dog was the most popular in the U.S.? [18]
  A. cocker spaniel
  B. German shepherd
  C. Labrador retriever
  D. poodle

Chapter 3

Entertainment, Literature, and Art

Answers to questions in this chapter begin on page 174.

True or False?

(1-Point Questions)

3.1 The 1989 box-office blockbuster *Batman* did not win any Academy awards. [39]

3.2 For a time, Gypsy Rose Lee, the famous stripper, moderated a TV quiz show called *Think Fast.* [28]

3.3 In the film *Who Framed Roger Rabbit?* the speaking and singing voices of the cartoon character Jessica Rabbit are performed by Kathleen Turner. [66]

3.4 In his last movie, Ronald Reagan portrayed a crime boss. [45]

3.5 In the 1942 animated film *Bambi*, Bambi is a female deer. [12]

3.6 The musical *The Music Man* is based on the life of composer Pyotr Ilyich Tchaikovsky. [32]

3.7 Bob Newhart once bought a Malibu beach house from Robert Redford. [61]

3.8 Verdi's opera *Aida*, set in Egypt, was commissioned to celebrate the opening of the Suez Canal. [22]

3.9 When Shakespeare's King Lear spoke of "a thankless child," he was talking about his son. [70]

3.10 The novel *First Blood*, the basis for the first Rambo film, was written by a former American Literature professor at the University of Iowa. [42]

3.11 After the success of the "Sweet Valley High" series for girls 12 and up, author Francine Pascal created a new series of adult romance novels called "Sweet Valley Twins." [3]

3.12 The last James Bond book ever written by Ian Fleming was *License Renewed*. [16]

3.13 Not only was *The $64,000 Question* a television quiz show in the 1950s, but *The $64 Question* was a radio quiz show of the 1940s. [65]

3.14 Steve McQueen starred in the original 1958 version of the horror film *The Blob*. [35]

3.15 Stendhal, who wrote the classic novel *The Red and The Black* in 1830, also wrote an unfinished novel called *The Pink and the Green*, which appeared in English for the first time in the 1980s. [51]

3.16 In the definition of Nebula Award categories for science fiction writing, the "novelette" award is reserved for works that are shorter than novels but longer than novellas. [9]

3.17 Katharine Hepburn was the first woman ever to win two consecutive Academy Awards for best actress. [6]

3.18 Warren Beatty appeared in the 1959–63 TV series *The Many Loves of Dobie Gillis*, playing a character named Milton Armitage. [24]

3.19 Richard Chamberlain made a popular recording of the theme song from his 1960s dramatic series *Dr. Kildare*. [55]

3.20 The musical term "diminuendo" means "very slow." [75]

3.21 Antonin Dvořák didn't visit the Americas until 12 years after he wrote his symphony titled *From the New World*. [37]

3.22 Jane Austen, the author of *Pride and Prejudice*, was actually the pseudonym of Lady Catherine de Bourg. [2]

3.23 The words to the song "Auld Lang Syne" were written by Scottish poet Robert Burns. [71]

3.24 Angela Lansbury starred in the original Broadway production of *Mame*. [41]

3.25 The musical *A Funny Thing Happened on the Way to the Forum* is based on Shakespeare's *A Comedy of Errors*. [34]

Multiple Choice

(2-Point Questions)

3.26 "Springfield" is *not* the home town of which of these TV
shows' families? [47]
A. *The Donna Reed Show*
B. *Father Knows Best*
C. *The Simpsons*

3.27 Who reportedly said, after winning the 1988 Oscar
(awarded in 1989) for best actress, "I never thought I'd
have a nomination...I never thought anybody ever took
any of my pictures seriously." [73]
A. Cher
B. Jodie Foster
C. Shirley Maclaine

3.28 In 1990, which of these characters turned 40 years of
age? [8]
A. Charlie Brown
B. Bugs Bunny
C. Fred Flintstone

3.29 In what year did *Monty Python's Flying Circus* debut on
the BBC? [25]
A. 1959
B. 1969
C. 1979

3.30 What is Twyla Tharp best known as? [64]
A. actress
B. choreographer
C. singer

3.31 Raffi is known for writing and singing what? [46]
A. children's songs
B. New Age music
C. rap music

3.32 In the opera *Carmen,* what is the name of Carmen's lover? [18]
A. Don Jose
B. Don Juan
C. Don Pedro

3.33 What cartoon character created a controversy in a 1988 TV episode when he sniffed crushed flower petals in a way that some viewers claimed resembled cocaine snorting? [13]
A. Bugs Bunny
B. Mighty Mouse
C. Popeye

3.34 Van Williams played the same character, private eye Ken Madison, on two different TV series set in different cities. What were the series? [56]
A. *Bourbon Street Beat* and *Surfside Six*
B. *Hawaiian Eye* and *77 Sunset Strip*
C. *Magnum P.I.* and *Simon & Simon*

3.35 The French playwrights Racine, Corneille, and Molière all lived during what century? [21]
A. 17th
B. 18th
C. 19th

3.36 Which soap opera left the air in early 1989 after more than 13 years? [74]
A. *Guiding Light*
B. *One Life to Live*
C. *Ryan's Hope*

3.37 From whom did Bugs Bunny borrow the lines "Here I am!" and "He don't know me very well, do he?" [10]
A. Milton Berle
B. Lou Costello
C. Red Skelton

3.38 When van Gogh's painting *Portrait of Dr. Gachet* was
sold in May 1990 to a representative of a Tokyo art
gallery, it set a record price for an auctioned work of art.
How much did it sell for? [62]
A. $825,000
B. $8,250,000
C. $82.5 million

3.39 Which Tom starred in *The Color of Money*? [30]
A. Tom Berenger
B. Tom Cruise
C. Tom Hanks

3.40 What is another name for a film crew's chief electrician?
[50]
A. big L
B. gaffer
C. sparks

3.41 According to the final episode of 1960s TV series *The
Fugitive*, who killed Dr. Richard Kimble's wife? [19]
A. a one-armed man
B. Kimble himself
C. Kimble's next-door neighbor

3.42 Who wrote the lyrics, "By the time we got to Woodstock,
we were half a million strong"? [59]
A. Judy Collins
B. David Crosby
C. Joni Mitchell

3.43 In what film are the names of the two main characters
Jack Walsh and Jonathan Mardukas? [44]
A. *Midnight Cowboy*
B. *Midnight Express*
C. *Midnight Run*

3.44 What network set a record by finishing first in weekly
prime-time ratings for a full year (52 consecutive weeks)
in 1988-89? [15]
A. ABC
B. CBS
C. NBC

3.45 Cuban-born pop star Gloria Estefan broke her back in 1990 in what kind of accident? [53]
   A. She fell off a stage.
   B. She was in a helicopter crash.
   C. A tractor-trailer collided with her tour bus.

3.46 What is the name of the robot in the 1951 science fiction film *The Day the Earth Stood Still*? [4]
   A. Gort
   B. Klaatu
   C. Robby

3.47 Where was actor Mel Gibson born? [68]
   A. Birmingham, England
   B. Peekskill, New York
   C. Wagga Wagga, Australia

3.48 In the 1980s, Susan Lucci was nominated 10 times for a daytime Emmy Award for her role as Erica Kane on *All My Children*. How many times did Susan Lucci win? [33]
   A. 0
   B. 5
   C. 10

3.49 In Charles Dickens's novel *A Tale of Two Cities*, what are the two cities? [49]
   A. Boston and New York
   B. London and Paris
   C. Rome and Venice

3.50 Three conductors of this U.S. city's orchestra have been Riccardo Muti, Eugene Ormandy, and Leopold Stokowski. What is the city? [1]
   A. Chicago
   B. Philadelphia
   C. New York

(3-Point Questions)

3.51 According to a *Forbes* magazine survey, what entertainer
was the highest paid for the two years 1988 and 1989
combined? [36]
  A. Bill Cosby
  B. Michael Jackson
  C. Madonna
  D. Oprah Winfrey

3.52 At first, Walt Disney's mouse creation wasn't called
Mickey. What was his original name? [58]
  A. Manville
  B. Melvin
  C. Mortimer
  D. Murgatroyd

3.53 What 17th-century soldier and writer wrote an early
science fiction work titled *Voyage to the Moon*? [29]
  A. Francis Bacon
  B. Cyrano de Bergerac
  C. René Descartes
  D. William Shakespeare

3.54 Actress Ava Gardner was married to all but which of the
following persons? [69]
  A. Richard Burton
  B. Mickey Rooney
  C. Frank Sinatra
  D. Artie Shaw

3.55 What symphony's last movement includes a setting of
Schiller's poem "Hymn to Joy"? [7]
  A. Beethoven's *Ninth*
  B. Bruckner's *Eighth*
  C. Mahler's *Tenth*
  D. Mozart's *40th*

3.56 What is Goldie Hawn's real first name? [20]
  A. Godiva
  B. Goldie
  C. Gloria
  D. Grace

3.57 In which movie did Clint Eastwood give us the immortal line, "Go ahead...make my day"? [43]

   A. *Dirty Harry*
   B. *Magnum Force*
   C. *Sudden Impact*
   D. *Tightrope*

3.58 What musical was based on Thornton Wilder's comedy *The Matchmaker*? [17]

   A. *Hello, Dolly!*
   B. *The Music Man*
   C. *Take Me Along*
   D. *The Unsinkable Molly Brown*

3.59 What bandleader was known as "the King of Swing"? [72]

   A. Tommy Dorsey
   B. Benny Goodman
   C. Guy Lombardo
   D. Glenn Miller

3.60 When this Eugene O'Neill play was revived on Broadway in 1988, Jason Robards and Colleen Dewhurst starred as James Tyrone and Mary Cavan Tyrone. What is the name of the play? [26]

   A. *Death of a Salesman*
   B. *The Iceman Cometh*
   C. *Long Day's Journey Into Night*
   D. *A Moon for the Misbegotten*

3.61 What kind of bird was the custodian of the secret word on the old quiz show *You Bet Your Life*? [57]

   A. a chicken
   B. a duck
   C. a goose
   D. a robin

3.62 According to *Gulliver's Travels*, in what year was Lemuel Gulliver shipwrecked on Lilliput? [40]

   A. 1599
   B. 1699
   C. 1799
   D. 1899

3.63 The mythical land of Narnia, created by the singing of the great lion Aslan, is featured in numerous works by which 20th century writer? [63]
A. L. Ron Hubbard
B. C.S. Lewis
C. H.P. Lovecraft
D. J.R.R. Tolkein

3.64 The French playwright Eugène Ionesco, known for his "absurd" plays, has called what other playwright—who was not a contemporary of Ionsesco's—"the King of the Theater of the Absurd"? [14]
A. Samuel Beckett
B. Molière
C. Jean-Paul Sartre
D. William Shakespeare

3.65 According to a Mark Twain novel, a mechanic from what New England state went back in time and visited King Arthur's court? [27]
A. Connecticut
B. Massachusetts
C. New Hampshire
D. Rhode Island

3.66 Mae West first spoke the line "Come up and see me sometime" in the 1933 film *She Done Him Wrong*. Who was her co-star in that movie? [52]
A. W.C. Fields
B. Cary Grant
C. James Stewart
D. John Wayne

3.67 On what TV series would you see a street gang called "the Sweathogs"? [38]
A. *Fame*
B. *Room 222*
C. *Welcome Back, Kotter*
D. *The White Shadow*

3.68 Whose autobiography was called *Back in the Saddle Again*? [67]
A. Gene Autry
B. Hopalong Cassidy
C. Tom Mix
D. Roy Rogers

3.69 In 1968, a Hugo Award for best science fiction dramatic presentation went to a TV series episode titled "City on the Edge of Forever." What was the name of the series? [5]
A. *Lost in Space*
B. *Science Fiction Theater*
C. *Star Trek*
D. *The Time Tunnel*

3.70 What was the first television show ever to be watched by over 50,000,000 households in the U.S.? [60]
A. Part VIII of *Roots* in 1977
B. the "Who Shot J.R?" episode of *Dallas* in 1980
C. the *M*A*S*H* special final episode in 1983
D. Super Bowl XX in 1986

3.71 *The Andy Griffith Show* was set in the little town of Mayberry. In what state was Mayberry? [31]
A. Georgia
B. Indiana
C. North Carolina
D. Tennessee

3.72 Which of the following writers was *not* also a doctor? [40]
A. Anton Chekhov
B. Somerset Maugham
C. Voltaire
D. William Carlos Williams

3.73 Which character in *Alice in Wonderland* is most often seen weeping? [11]
A. Bill the Lizard
B. the Dormouse
C. the Gryphon
D. the Mock Turtle

3.74 Which role did Jim Backus *not* play? [54]
   A. the cartoon voice of Mr. Magoo
   B. "I" on the '50s TV series *I Married Joan.*
   C. Thurston Howell III on the '60s TV series *Gilligan's Island*
   D. the voice of Charlie on the '70s TV series *Charlie's Angels*

3.75 Which of the following persons wrote some of the *Flash Gordon* comic strips that appeared in Europe during World War II? [23]
   A. Buster Crabbe
   B. Charles DeGaulle
   C. Federico Fellini
   D. Hermann Hesse

Chapter 4

Geography and Sightseeing

Answers to questions in this chapter begin on page 176.

True or False?

(1-Point Questions)

4.1 In area, Yellowstone is the largest National Park in the United States. [30]

4.2 The Seattle Space Needle is taller than any other building in Seattle. [73]

4.3 Paris, France, is farther north than Montreal, Canada. [8]

4.4 On the average, the Atlantic Ocean is deeper than the Pacific Ocean. [28]

4.5 New Delhi is the capital and largest city of India. [62]

4.6 The Malvinas Islands and the Falkland Islands are one and the same. [15]

4.7 The northernmost point of mainland Scandinavia is in Norway. [36]

4.8 There are more provinces in Canada than there are republics in the Soviet Union. [11]

4.9 The island of Alcatraz gets its name from the Spanish word for "pelican." [56]

4.10 It's possible to ride up inside St. Louis's Gateway Arch in an elevator. [31]

4.11 In the U.S., most state capitals are also the largest cities (in population) in their state. [47]

4.12 The highest point in South Carolina is farther above sea level than the highest point in Kansas. [74]

4.13 Sequoia National Park and Redwood National Park are one and the same. [60]

4.14 In area, England is larger than New England. [7]

4.15 As the crow flies, Honolulu is closer to Tokyo than it is to New York City. [66]

4.16 Detroit, Michigan is in the same time zone as Indianapolis, Indiana. [6]

4.17 In area, Antarctica is the smallest continent. [45]

4.18 The Iberian peninsula comprises the countries of Portugal and Spain. [17]

4.19 The Dead Sea is the lowest point in the world, lying over 1,300 feet below sea level. [55]

4.20 The northern tip of Antarctica comes closer to the equator than the southern tip of Greenland. [27]

4.21 Afghanistan borders the Indian Ocean. [63]

4.22 It is impossible to reach any part of Mexico by traveling due north from any part of South America. [34]

4.23 In area, Canada was larger than the U.S. until Alaska became a state, but now the U.S. is larger. [54]

4.24 London is closer to Berlin than New York is to Chicago. [25]

4.25 No two U.S. states that border one another have names beginning with the same letter of the alphabet. [67]

(2-Point Questions)

4.26 Asia's Himalaya Mountains are the highest in the world. But what continent has the highest point outside of Asia? [37]
  A. Africa
  B. North America
  C. South America

4.27 What country completely owns three of the 10 largest islands in the world? [72]
  A. Canada
  B. Indonesia
  C. Japan

4.28 Goat Island, Luna Island, and Three Sisters Island can all be found near what major tourist attraction? [49]
  A. Disney World
  B. Niagara Falls
  C. the Statue of Liberty

4.29 Despite its name, the Caspian Sea is considered to be the largest lake in the world. What lake is the next largest? [20]
  A. Great Slave Lake
  B. Lake Superior
  C. Lake Victoria

4.30 Not counting Lake Superior, which of the Great Lakes is the largest? [61]
  A. Lake Erie
  B. Lake Huron
  C. Lake Michigan

4.31 When it's midnight in the westernmost point of the Soviet Union, what time is it in the easternmost point of the Soviet Union? [9]
  A. 5 a.m.
  B. 10 a.m.
  C. 5 p.m.

4.32 The Pyrenees Mountains are located along the border of France and which of these countries? [41]
  A. Belgium
  B. Spain
  C. Switzerland

4.33 How much does Plymouth Rock weigh? [18]
  A. 4 tons
  B. 40 tons
  C. 400 tons

4.34 The National Cowboy Hall of Fame and Western Heritage Center overlooks the Chisolm Trail in what city? [33]
  A. Cheyenne, Wyoming
  B. Dodge City, Kansas
  C. Oklahoma City, Oklahoma

4.35 What is Mount Erebus? [57]
   A. an active volcano in Antarctica
   B. an underwater peak off Greece that is a hazard to Mediterranean shipping
   C. a nearly 17,000-foot peak on the Iran-Turkey border, where Noah's Ark may have landed

4.36 What was the first National Monument established in the U.S.? [3]
   A. Devils Tower
   B. Dinosaur
   C. Joshua Tree

4.37 Which of the following countries does *not* border the Yellow Sea? [46]
   A. China
   B. Japan
   C. Korea

4.38 The Daniel Boone home, where he died, has been made a museum. How is it best described? [69]
   A. a log cabin in Kentucky
   B. a two-story clapboard house in Tennessee
   C. a four-story Georgian-style house in Missouri

4.39 Where is Fort Duquesne? [22]
   A. Cincinnati
   B. Detroit
   C. Pittsburgh

4.40 The Alamo, site of a famous 1836 battle, is now a tourist attraction in the heart of what Texas city? [39]
   A. Austin
   B. Houston
   C. San Antonio

4.41 The Brenner Pass connects Austria and which other country? [51]
   A. Hungary
   B. Italy
   C. Switzerland

4.42 Which New England state does *not* border the Atlantic ocean? [12]
   A. Maine
   B. New Hampshire
   C. Vermont

4.43 Ulan Bator is the capital of what country? [32]
   A. Madagascar
   B. Mali
   C. Mongolia

4.44 Where is the Iwo Jima Memorial statue? [75]
   A. Arlington, Virginia
   B. the island of Iwo Jima
   C. Washington. D.C.

4.45 McCormick Place, the largest temporary exhibition facility in North America, overlooks Lake Michigan in what city? [16]
   A. Chicago
   B. Detroit
   C. Milwaukee

4.46 In passing through the Panama Canal from the Atlantic (via the Caribbean Sea) to the Pacific, what is the approximate direction a ship travels? [5]
   A. northwest
   B. southeast
   C. southwest

4.47 The ski resorts of Snowbird, Alta, and Park City are close to what city? [43]
   A. Montpelier, Vermont
   B. Denver, Colorado
   C. Salt Lake City, Utah

4.48 Which European capital city lies at the mouth of the Liffey River? [65]
   A. Amsterdam
   B. Copenhagen
   C. Dublin

4.49 The Bingham Canyon Copper Mine, America's largest man-made excavation, is near U.S. routes 15 and 80 in what state? [26]
A. California
B. Nevada
C. Utah

4.50 What is the capital of the American Virgin Islands? [13]
A. Agana
B. Charlotte Amalie
C. Pago Pago

(3-Point Questions)

4.51 George Washington's face is carved in granite at Mount Rushmore National Memorial, along with the faces of all but which of the following presidents? [70]
A. Andrew Jackson
B. Thomas Jefferson
C. Abraham Lincoln
D. Theodore Roosevelt

4.52 What U.S. city, nicknamed the "Athens of the South," contains a full-scale replica of the ancient Parthenon? [38]
A. Columbia, South Carolina
B. Memphis, Tennessee
C. Nashville, Tennessee
D. New Orleans, Louisiana

4.53 Which U.S. national park regularly has the most visitors each year? [23]
A. Great Smoky Mountains
B. Grand Canyon
C. Yellowstone
D. Yosemite

4.54 The Biblical city of Babylon would be in what country today? [53]
A. Iran
B. Iraq
C. Israel
D. Jordan

4.55 Which of the following is *not* an African country? [44]
A. Zaire
B. Zambia
C. Zambesia
D. Zimbabwe

4.56 East of the Mississippi River, what state has the largest area? [1]
A. Florida
B. Georgia
C. Illinois
D. Michigan

4.57 Which of the following countries does *not* border Israel? [40]
A. Egypt
B. Jordan
C. Saudi Arabia
D. Syria

4.58 Which of the following U.S. cities is *not* a state capital? [10]
A. Atlanta
B. Baltimore
C. Boston
D. Honolulu

4.59 Tenerife is the largest island of which group? [71]
A. the Balearics
B. the Canarys
C. the Falklands
D. the Galapagos

4.60 The Sultan Ahmet Mosque, also known as the Blue Mosque due to magnificent blue tiles in its interior, is said to be the only mosque in the world with six minarets. Where is it? [19]
A. Cairo, Egypt
B. Istanbul, Turkey
C. Los Angeles, California
D. Mecca, Saudi Arabia

4.61 Excluding Alaska, which U.S. state extends the farthest
north? [48]
   A. Maine
   B. Michigan
   C. Minnesota
   D. Washington

4.62 What function is served by the Paris building known as
the Sorbonne? [29]
   A. hospital
   B. museum
   C. school
   D. theater

4.63 In what African country is the Central Kalahari Game
Reserve?[58]
   A. Botswana
   B. Kenya
   C. Nigeria
   D. South Africa

4.64 The Breakers, a 70-room mansion built in the 1890s by
Cornelius Vanderbilt, was once the largest house in the
United States. Where is it? [24]
   A. Newport, Rhode Island
   B. Philadelphia, Pennsylvania
   C. Richmond, Virginia
   D. San Francisco, California

4.65 Which is not a state of Australia? [50]
   A. Northern Australia
   B. Queensland
   C. Tasmania
   D. Victoria

4.66 Which of the following is *not* known as one of the Baltic
states? [35]
   A. Albania
   B. Estonia
   C. Latvia
   D. Lithuania

4.67 The Lincoln Park Zoological Garden, established in
1868, is said to be the oldest zoo in the United States. In
what city is it located? [64]
A. Chicago
B. Philadelphia
C. New York
D. Washington

4.68 If you could dig a straight line from Kansas through the
center of the earth, and continue out the other side of the
world, where would you come out? [4]
A. Australia
B. Indonesia
C. the southern Indian Ocean
D. the South Pacific, near New Zealand

4.69 How many of the five Great Lakes border only one state?
[42]
A. 0
B. 1
C. 2
D. 3

4.70 What is the only state that has no point as high as 400 feet
above sea level? [14]
A. Delaware
B. Florida
C. Louisiana
D. Rhode Island

4.71 The most recorded deaths from a volcanic eruption
occurred when Mt. Pelée erupted, killing 40,000 persons.
On what island is Mt. Pelée? [68]
A. Hawaii
B. Java
C. Martinique
D. Sicily

4.72 Lake Victoria, Africa's largest lake, is nestled between
three nations. Which of these is *not* one of those nations?
[2]
A. Kenya
B. Tanzania
C. Uganda
D. Zaire

4.73 By air, which of the following pairs of major world cities
are fewer than 5,000 miles apart? [52]
A. Cape Town and London
B. Hong Kong and Honolulu
C. Mexico City and Paris
D. Moscow and Washington

4.74 By air, which of the following pairs of major world cities
are more than 10,000 miles apart? [21]
A. Honolulu and Paris
B. London and Tokyo
C. Moscow and New York
D. Rio de Janeiro and Hong Kong

4.75 In 1988, 18- to 24-year-olds from which of the following
countries had the worst average score in an international
geography test given by the National Geographic Society
and the Gallup Organization? [59]
A. France
B. Mexico
C. Sweden
D. United States

Chapter 5

History and Demographics

Answers to questions in this chapter begin on page 178.

True or False?

(1-Point Questions)

5.1 John F. Kennedy was the first president to name his brother to a cabinet post. [22]

5.2 The British rulers William III and Mary II, better known as William and Mary, were not only married but were first cousins. [9]

5.3 In the U.S., there were fewer people aged 15-19 in 1990 than in 1980. [41]

5.4 No U.S. First Lady, or former First Lady, has ever lived to be older than Bess Truman. [18]

5.5 The 1989 oil spill into Prince William Sound by the Exxon tanker *Valdez* was the largest oil spill in U.S. history. [50]

5.6 Switzerland and the United States both joined the United Nations in the year it was founded, 1945. [33]

5.7 Alexander Hamilton killed Aaron Burr in a duel. [20]

5.8 In 1948, Albert Einstein was offered the presidency of Israel. [14]

5.9 The first Purple Heart was awarded during the American Revolution. [48]

5.10 In 1598, the Edict of Nantes outlawed the Protestant religion in France. [61]

5.11 David Dinkins was the first black person to be elected mayor of New York City. [51]

5.12 A person born with the name Leslie Lynch King, Jr. was once president of the United States. [71]

5.13 During the 1980s, the average household size in the U.S. decreased. [46]

5.14 The Hundred Years War, fought between England and France, was so called because it lasted exactly 100 years. [30]

5.15 The ancient city of Pompeii was destroyed by the eruption of Mount Vesuvius. [68]

5.16 Abraham Lincoln was the first president of the United States to sport a beard. [7]

5.17 Despite legend, General Custer actually survived his "last stand," the Battle of Little Big Horn. [63]

5.18 More than half the delegates to the 1988 Democratic Convention were women. [31]

5.19 The 16th-century explorer Giovanni da Verrazano, for whom the Verrazano Bridge in New York City was named, never explored farther north than Virginia. [54]

5.20 Brian Mulroney's immediate predecessor as prime minister of Canada was Pierre Trudeau. [35]

5.21 For a time, the Egyptian queen Cleopatra lived in Rome with Julius Caesar. [2]

5.22 Running for reelection as governor of Massachusetts in 1978, Michael Dukakis lost the Democratic primary to Edward King, a former pro football player. [56]

5.23 In 1818, Congress reduced the number of stripes on the U.S. flag from 15 to 13. [62]

5.24 Theodore Roosevelt was the first president to ride in an automobile. [4]

5.25 When the 20th century began, the British monarch was Queen Victoria. [69]

Multiple Choice

(2-Point Questions)

5.26 What percentage of eligible voters voted in the 1988 U.S. presidential election? [40]
A. 30%
B. 50%
C. 70%

5.27 History students are taught about "the fall of Constantinople" in 1453. To whom did it fall? [60]
A. Christian crusaders
B. Mongol hordes
C. Ottoman Turks

5.28 John Brown of Civil War fame was which? [12]
  A. an abolitionist
  B. a slave
  C. a slave-owner

5.29 As of mid 1990, which group of elected officials
  contained the highest percentage of women? [65]
  A. state governors
  B. state legislators
  C. U.S. Congress

5.30 From whom are the Creoles of today's New Orleans
  descended? [37]
  A. French-Canadians from Nova Scotia
  B. French and Spanish settlers who lived in the city
  C. refugees from the Crimean War

5.31 He is called "the Father of Our Country." But how many
  children did George Washington actually have? [25]
  A. 0
  B. 3
  C. 7

5.32 Two of the following states declined in population from
  1980 to 1990. Which one's population grew? [10]
  A. Iowa
  B. West Virginia
  C. Vermont

5.33 Which of these three wise men died before the other two
  were born? [53]
  A. Confucius
  B. Plato
  C. Solomon

5.34 In what year did the Peace Corps have its greatest number
  of volunteers? [29]
  A. 1966
  B. 1976
  C. 1986

5.35 Which of these names has *not* been a previous name of the city of Leningrad? [57]
   A. Petrograd
   B. St. Petersburg
   C. Stalingrad

5.36 Which two states became states on the same day? [5]
   A. North and South Carolina
   B. North and South Dakota
   C. Virginia and West Virginia

5.37 In what year did the Census Bureau first report that a majority of new mothers were remaining in the job market? [45]
   A. 1968
   B. 1978
   C. 1988

5.38 During what war did Florence Nightingale become known as "the Lady With the Lamp"? [16]
   A. American Civil War
   B. Crimean War
   C. World War I

5.39 What did the "J" stand for in "J. Edgar Hoover"? [75]
   A. James
   B. John
   C. Joseph

5.40 How many people were killed when Mt. St. Helens erupted on May 18, 1980? [8]
   A. 1
   B. 57
   C. 571

5.41 Which of these centuries was part of the Ming Dynasty in China? [74]
   A. 5th century B.C.
   B. 5th century A.D.
   C. 15th century A.D.

5.42 In 1990, what state's population had the youngest median age? [15]
A. Alaska
B. Hawaii
C. Utah

5.43 In 1990, what state's population had the oldest median age? [58]
A. Florida
B. New York
C. North Dakota

5.44 Whom did Violeta Barrios de Chamorro defeat in a 1989 presidential election? [26]
A. Alfredo Cristiani
B. Daniel Ortega
C. Jose Sarney

5.45 Approximately how long had Nelson Mandela been imprisoned in South Africa before he was freed in 1990? [67]
A. 7 years
B. 17 years
C. 27 years

5.46 What job did Secretary of Defense Dick Cheney hold before becoming George Bush's Secretary of Defense? [42]
A. congressman from Wyoming
B. governor of New Hampshire
C. secretary of defense under Ronald Reagan

5.47 Czechosolvakia is made up of two main ethnic groups, Chechs and Slovaks. In that country, which of the following is true?[3]
A. Czechs outnumber Slovaks about two to one.
B. Slovaks outnumber Czechs about two to one.
C. There are roughly equal numbers of Czechs and Slovaks.

5.48 Who preceded William Rehnquist as chief justice of the Supreme Court? [55]
A. Warren Burger
B. Abe Fortas
C. Earl Warren

5.49 What city became the first capital of the United States in January 1785, when the Congress of Confederation met at its City Hall? [73]
A. Boston
B. New York City
C. Philadelphia

5.50 In 1990, in what percentage of U.S. married couples did the wife earn more money than the husband? [21]
A. 18
B. 38
C. 58

(3-Point Questions)

5.51 In 1965, what future president wrote an autobiography titled *Where's the Rest of Me*? [44]
A. Jimmy Carter
B. Gerald Ford
C. Richard Nixon
D. Ronald Reagan

5.52 In what year did the population of the United States increase the most—a record 3.1 million? [36]
A. 1956
B. 1966
C. 1976
D. 1986

5.53 What country did Catherine the Great rule? [72]
A. England
B. France
C. Germany
D. Russia

5.54 What were the first names of explorers Lewis and Clark? [38]
    A. Benjamin and Samuel
    B. Clark and Lewis
    C. John and Lincoln
    D. Meriwether and William

5.55 In World War I, which of the following countries was *not* one of Germany's allies? [23]
    A. Austria-Hungary
    B. Bulgaria
    C. Italy
    D. Turkey (the Ottoman Empire)

5.56 The average population density of the U.S. is approximately how many persons per square mile? [28]
    A. 35
    B. 70
    C. 100
    D. 150

5.57 What did the "D" in "D-Day" stand for? [66]
    A. day
    B. doom
    C. Dunkirk
    D. Dwight (Eisenhower)

5.58 Which of these four U.S. presidents served his term before the other three? [24]
    A. Millard Fillmore
    B. James Polk
    C. Zachary Taylor
    D. John Tyler

5.59 The erroneous 1948 headline "Dewey Defeats Truman" was printed on the front page of which newspaper? [47]
    A. *Chicago Tribune*
    B. *New York Times*
    C. *San Francisco Chronicle*
    D. *Washington Post*

5.60 David, the Biblical king of "David and Goliath" fame,
was alive during which of the following years? [64]
A. 3001 B.C.
B. 2001 B.C.
C. 1001 B.C.
D. 1 B.C.

5.61 After the original 13 states, what was the next state
admitted to the United States? [59]
A. Florida
B. Kentucky
C. Vermont
D. West Virginia

5.62 Which of these events did *not* occur in the year 1876? [17]
A. Alexander Graham Bell invented the telephone.
B. Baseball's National League was founded.
C. Colorado became a state.
D. Stanley found Livingstone.

5.63 Of the first 40 presidents of the United States, how many
were not yet 50 years old when they were sworn in? [1]
A. 3
B. 6
C. 12
D. 24

5.64 The Third Reich ended when Germany surrendered in
1945. When did the Second Reich end? [52]
A. 1453
B. 1871
C. 1918
D. 1933

5.65 In whose embassy did General Manuel Noriega take
refuge after the U.S. invasion of Panama City in 1989?
[32]
A. Cuba
B. Nicaragua
C. Switzerland
D. Vatican City

5.66 Three of these events happened in 1985. Which one took place in 1982? [39]
  A. Mikhail Gorbachev became the leader of the Soviet Union.
  B. Pete Rose broke Ty Cobb's record of 4,191 career hits.
  C. Coca Cola replaced its formula to create a "new" Coke.
  D. Britain and Argentina fought a war over the Falkland Islands.

5.67 Namibia, which achieved independence from South Africa in 1990, became a colony of what European nation in 1890, under the name South-West Africa? [70]
  A. Germany
  B. Great Britain
  C. The Netherlands
  D. Portugal

5.68 What frontier marshall was murdered in 1876 in Deadwood, South Dakota, by outlaw Jack McCall? [6]
  A. Buffalo Bill Cody
  B. Matt Dillon
  C. Wild Bill Hickok
  D. Bat Masterson

5.69 Leonard Kristensen of Norway led the first party to land on the mainland of Antarctica. What was the year? [34]
  A. 1795
  B. 1845
  C. 1895
  D. 1945

5.70 For years on this island nation, formerly known as Ceylon, Tamil separatists have been conducting attacks against the Sinhalese majority. What is the name of the country? [13]
  A. Cyprus
  B. Madagascar
  C. Seychelles
  D. Sri Lanka

5.71 Which American commander said, "I have not yet begun
to fight"? [49]
   A. George Dewey
   B. David Farragut
   C. John Paul Jones
   D. Oliver Hazard Perry

5.72 Just before the Civil War, approximately what was the
average life expectancy of white males born in the U.S.?
[19]
   A. 40 years
   B. 50 years
   C. 60 years
   D. 70 years

5.73 In what state have the most U.S. presidents been born?
[27]
   A. Massachusetts
   B. New York
   C. Ohio
   D. Virginia

5.74 Where were the United Nations' headquarters located
before they moved to Manhattan's East Side? [43]
   A. San Francisco
   B. suburban Long Island, New York
   C. Geneva, Switzerland
   D. Paris, France

5.75 At the time of the Declaration of Independence, what was
the approximate population of the United States? [11]
   A. 20,000
   B. 200,000
   C. 2,000,000
   D. 20,000,000

Chapter 6

Science and Nature

Answers to questions in this chapter begin on page 181.

True or False?

(1-Point Questions)

6.1 Parrots sometimes live to be over 100 years old. [47]

6.2 Pasteurization kills all the bacteria in milk. [7]

6.3 The habit of "cracking your knuckles" can cause arthritis. [63]

6.4 Swimming typically burns more calories than aerobic dancing. [49]

6.5 When the moon is at its "first quarter," it appears to have about a quarter the area of a full moon. [57]

6.6 Pacific salmon all die after spawning, but some Atlantic salmon live to spawn more than once. [12]

6.7 Dry ice is the solid form of carbon dioxide. [26]

6.8 Radio waves travel faster than x-rays. [51]

6.9 Generally, if a man and a woman of the same weight drink the same amount of alcohol, the woman will feel the effect more. [58]

6.10 A vampire bat will sometimes consume its own body weight in blood in a single night. [42]

6.11 Nitrous oxide is also known as tear gas. [15]

6.12 Though slow moving, most box turtles migrate more than 100 miles during a single year. [60]

6.13 Poison ivy can be caught from someone who has it. [27]

6.14 Hydrogen can become a liquid if it is made cold enough, but it will never freeze solid. [72]

6.15 The acid that gives you "acid indigestion" is hydrochloric acid. [33]

6.16 Through 1990, no woman astronaut or cosmonaut had ever "walked in space." [1]

6.17 The letter K is the symbol for the chemical element krypton. [65]

6.18 A sponge is a plant that feeds on tiny organic material found in sea water. [44]

6.19 Steroid hormones can cause glaucoma. [29]

6.20 In the human body, the liver is larger than the stomach. [14]

6.21 Most monkeys can differentiate colors just as well as humans. [62]

6.22 Sound travels faster through the air than underwater. [74]

6.23 Elephants usually live longer than humans. [55]

6.24 Rocks from the moon sometimes find their way to earth as meteorites. [37]

6.25 Although their name means "100-legged," most centipedes have fewer than 50 legs. [18]

Multiple Choice

(2-Point Questions)

6.26 The University of California successfully bred which two different species of animals? [23]
A. a goat and a sheep, producing a new animal called a "geep"
B. a horse and a camel, producing a new animal called a "hormel"
C. a rabbit and a hamster, producing a new animal called a "ramster"

6.27 Which of the following contains the fewest calories? [43]
A. 5 ounces of beer
B. 5 ounces of whole milk
C. 5 teaspoons of sugar

6.28 What is a shaddock? [53]
A. a crystal, such as quartz, that sticks out from a mineral vein
B. a fish, the offspring of a male shad and a female haddock.
C. a grapefruit

6.29 At what temperature, in degrees Fahrenheit, should meat be kept frozen? [48]
A. 0 degrees or below
B. between 10 and 20 degrees
C. around 30 degrees

94

The Original Trivia Treasury

6.30 The scapula is the more formal name for what? [4]
  A. the shoulder blade
  B. the thigh bone
  C. the wrist bone

6.31 Until 1977, Saturn was the only planet known to have rings. Since then, at least one ring has been found around which other planet or planets? [59]
  A. Jupiter, Uranus, and Neptune
  B. Uranus and Neptune only
  C. Uranus only

6.32 Which of these animals usually weighs the least? [28]
  A. lions
  B. tigers
  C. polar bears

6.33 Which of these instruments is used to measure the humidity? [36]
  A. anemometer
  B. barometer
  C. hygrometer

6.34 Which of these drugs was discovered first? [17]
  A. aspirin
  B. cocaine
  C. penicillin

6.35 The spacecraft *Magellan*, launched from the space shuttle *Atlantis* in 1989, was sent to map the surface of what planet? [67]
  A. Mars
  B. Neptune
  C. Venus

6.36 When it went into operation in 1989, the LEP—or Large Electron-Positron Collider, a circular tunnel 16.6 miles in circumference—was the largest scientific instrument ever built. Where is it? [41]
  A. Austria and Germany
  B. California and Nevada
  C. France and Switzerland

6.37 What makes Mexican jumping beans "jump"? [22]
A. larvae of a moth, reacting to the warmth in the hand of someone holding the bean
B. movement of a small but heavy kernel within the bean
C. They don't—it's a myth.

6.38 How long ago did dinosaurs become extinct? [5]
A. 600,000 years
B. 6 million years
C. 60 million years

6.39 Some scientists believe that certain kinds of dinosaurs did not become extinct, but instead evolved into what modern-day creatures? [19]
A. amphibians
B. birds
C. reptiles

6.40 Which vaccine was developed by Louis Pasteur? [64]
A. polio
B. rabies
C. smallpox

6.41 According to Ice Age patterns of the last half million years, when is the next Ice Age due to arrive? [39]
A. sometime in the next 2,000 years—possibly quite soon
B. sometime between 10,000 and 20,000 years from now
C. sometime between 100,000 and 200,000 years from now

6.42 In computer software, how many bits are in a kilobyte? [52]
A. 1,000
B. 8,000
C. 8,192

6.43 What causes the disease toxoplasmosis? [8]
A. a bacterium
B. a protozoan
C. a virus

6.44 Which kinds of camels have two humps: Arabian (also
known as dromedary) or Bactrian? [31]
   A. Arabian camels only
   B. Bactrian camels only
   C. some Arabian camels and some Bactrian camels

6.45 According to relativity theory, if a spaceship accelerated
to near the speed of light, a stationary observer off the
ship might notice all but which of the following? [45]
   A. Clocks on the ship would slow down.
   B. The ship would get smaller.
   C. The ship would lose mass.

6.46 In which kind of geometry is the sum of the angles inside
a triangle exactly equal to 180 degrees? [25]
   A. elliptical
   B. Euclidean
   C. hyperbolic

6.47 Which of these minerals can most easily scratch the other
two? [9]
   A. garnet
   B. quartz
   C. topaz

6.48 During a lunar eclipse, which of the following is true?
[69]
   A. The earth is between the sun and the moon.
   B. The moon is between the earth and the sun.
   C. The sun is between the earth and the moon.

6.49 If a square and a circle have the same area, then which
must be true? [16]
   A. The circle's circumference is equal to the square's
perimeter.
   B. The circle's circumference is greater than the
square's perimeter.
   C. The circle's circumference is less than the square's
perimeter.

6.50 According to theory, what kinds of quarks form the protons and neutrons in the atoms of ordinary matter? [38]
A. strange and charmed
B. top and bottom
C. up and down

(3-Point Questions)

6.51 Which is *not* considered to be one of the primary colors of light? [71]
A. red
B. yellow
C. green
D. blue

6.52 In 1989, Norwegian scientists found that there are far more viruses in oceans, lakes, and streams than previously believed. How many viruses did they find that a single milliliter of natural water may contain? [54]
A. up to 250
B. up to 25,000
C. up to 2,500,000
D. up to 250,000,000

6.53 Which pair of planets is most similar in size—that is, in which pair is the ratio of the diameters closest to 1? [21]
A. Mars and Mercury
B. Jupiter and Saturn
C. Uranus and Neptune
D. Venus and Earth

6.54 According to the Saffir-Simpson scale, what is the slowest windspeed a hurricane can have? [73]
A. 50 m.p.h.
B. 74 m.p.h.
C. 96 m.p.h.
D. 110 m.p.h.

6.55 Which of these mammals, on the average, has the shortest lifespan? [56]
   A. gray squirrel
   B. grizzly bear
   C. kangaroo
   D. moose

6.56 In what decade was television invented? [6]
   A. 1920s
   B. 1930s
   C. 1940s
   D. 1950s

6.57 Which of these has been referred to as the "disease of kings"? [35]
   A. hemophilia
   B. jaundice
   C. rubella
   D. syphilis

6.58 Which of these flowers did not derive its name by adding "ia" to the last name of a botanist? [61]
   A. fuchsia
   B. magnolia
   C. petunia
   D. zinnia

6.59 W.C. Roentgen was awarded the first Nobel prize in physics for what discovery? [46]
   A. inertia
   B. magnetism
   C. quantum theory
   D. x-rays

6.60 What is the most likely thing someone would do with the compound $MgSO_4 \cdot 7H_2O$? [75]
   A. blow up a building
   B. fertilize a lawn
   C. power a car
   D. soak one's feet

6.61 Which of these mammals lays eggs? [10]
   A. kangaroo
   B. koala
   C. platypus
   D. Tasmanian devil

6.62 In January 1990, what became the third nation on Earth, after the U.S. and Soviet Union, to launch a spacecraft to the moon? [70]
   A. China
   B. France
   C. Japan
   D. United Kingdom

6.63 If a hertz is equal to one cycle per second, how many cycles per second does a megahertz equal? [50]
   A. 1/1,000
   B. 1,000
   C. 1,000,000
   D. 1,000,000,000

6.64 No spacecraft from Earth has ever landed on which of the following? [2]
   A. Jupiter
   B. Mars
   C. the moon
   D. Venus

6.65 What is the name of the eye disease in which a buildup of fluid causes pressure inside the eyeball to increase, damaging the optic nerve at the back of the eye? [30]
   A. astigmatism
   B. cataract
   C. glaucoma
   D. retinitis

6.66 Of the eight other known planets in the solar system, how many are smaller than Earth? [11]
   A. 0
   B. 2
   C. 4
   D. 6

6.67 What gas accounts for about 78 percent of the earth's
atmosphere? [66]
A. argon
B. carbon dioxide
C. nitrogen
D. oxygen

6.68 In what century were the greatest number of chemical
elements discovered? [34]
A. 17th
B. 18th
C. 19th
D. 20th

6.69 In chemistry, what element is represented by the symbol
C? [20]
A. calcium
B. carbon
C. chlorine
D. copper

6.70 In research related to purifying air in space stations,
NASA scientists found that philodendrons help remove
all but which of these pollutants from the air? [3]
A. benzene
B. carbon monoxide
C. formaldehyde
D. radon

6.71 What is an imaginary number? [32]
A. any complex number
B. any irrational number
C. the result of dividing any number by zero
D. the square root of any negative real number

6.72 On what plant, which can take over 100 years to flower
and produce seeds naturally, were flowers first produced
in a laboratory in 1990? [13]
A. bamboo
B. coffee
C. pink dogwood
D. rubber tree

6.73 Amperes, or amps, are a unit of measure of what? [40]
  A. electric charge
  B. electric current
  C. electric field strength
  D. electric potential

6.74 The first manned U.S. Space Shuttle flight took place in April, 1981. What was the name of that shuttle? [24]
  A. *Atlantis*
  B. *Columbia*
  C. *Challenger*
  D. *Discovery*

6.75 Which principle explains both why hot food cools off and why cold food warms up when put at room temperature? [68]
  A. chemical equilibrium
  B. entropy
  C. momentum
  D. relativity

Chapter 7

Sports and Games

Answers to questions in this chapter begin on page 183.

True or False?

(1-Point Questions)

7.1 A regulation basketball outweighs a regulation soccer ball. [14]

7.2 In international competition, left-footed figure skaters must perform their routines in a clockwise direction around the rink, while right-footed skaters must go counterclockwise. [63]

7.3 It is illegal to place a bet at a Japanese horseracing track. [40]

7.4 In major league baseball, both the Minnesota Twins and the Texas Rangers were previously known as the Washington Senators. [57]

7.5 In terms of number of men on the field at one time, a Canadian football team outnumbers an American football team. [26]

7.6 Auto racers Al Unser and Bobby Unser are first cousins. [72]

7.7 If a tennis player hits the ball over the net with so much backspin that the ball bounces back across the net, the opponent is allowed to reach over the net with his or her racket to hit the ball. [17]

7.8 The course for the Tour de France bicycle race is always entirely within France. [43]

7.9 Although he led the American League in home runs many times, Babe Ruth never led the league in batting average. [20]

7.10 Harvard once won the Rose Bowl football game. [7]

7.11 The curved line that marks the three-point range on an NBA basketball court gets closer to the basket near the corners of the court. [69]

7.12 Although a few great pitchers have won over 300 games in their major league careers, no major leaguer has ever lost over 300 games. [29]

7.13 Although he was basketball's all-time leading scorer, Kareem Abdul-Jabbar never made a three-pointer. [58]

7.14 It is impossible for a pitcher to get credit for a perfect game if one of his teammates commits an error during the game. [36]

7.15 Triple Crown winner Secretariat was unable to have offspring. [1]

7.16 Mike Tyson was the youngest heavyweight champion in the history of boxing when he first won the title. [49]

7.17 Kathy Whitworth won more professional golf tournaments than any male player. [33]

7.18 When 19-year-old Gertrude Ederle swam the English
      Channel on August 6, 1926, she was not only the first
      woman to do it, but her time broke the men's record. [68]

7.19 No major league baseball player has ever struck out more
      than 100 times in a season in which he led his league in
      batting average. [4]

7.20 At the 1988 Olympics, identical twins represented the
      United States in the sport of synchronized swimming. [53]

7.21 In poker, if a joker is used as a wild card, a straight flush
      beats four of a kind but loses to five of a kind. [15]

7.22 Throughout baseball history, the most common nickname
      among players has been "Red." [44]

7.23 In his first four Super Bowl games (through 1990), Joe
      Montana never threw an intercepted pass. [59]

7.24 When Jennifer Capriati turned pro in 1990, she became
      the youngest U.S. female tennis player ever to have done
      so. [19]

7.25 When Shoeless Joe Jackson of the Chicago White Sox
      was tried for attempting to "defraud the public" by
      throwing the 1919 World Series to Cincinnati, a jury
      found him innocent. [50]

Multiple Choice

(2-Point Questions)

7.26 Who invented lacrosse? [30]
      A. American Indians
      B. Basques
      C. French Canadians

7.27 For an outdoor 100-meter dash result to count as a record, what is the fastest the wind speed may be? [62]
A. one international foot per second.
B. two meters per second
C. There is no official limit.

7.28 In standard darts, what is the most points that can be scored with a single dart? [10]
A. 50
B. 60
C. 100

7.29 If a bookmaker lists the odds on a baseball game as 8 to 5, how much would you have to bet on the favorite in order to win $5? [74]
A. $6.50
B. $8
C. $13

7.30 During the 1980s, Wayne Gretzky won the National Hockey League's most valuable player award, the Hart Trophy, nine times out of 10. Who won it the other time? [21]
A. Ray Bourque
B. Mario Lemieux
C. Patrick Roy

7.31 Which of these players received the highest percentage of votes for election to the Baseball Hall of Fame? [56]
A. Hank Aaron
B. Ty Cobb
C. Babe Ruth

7.32 In awarding points for team standings, the English League has rules that are different from other soccer leagues. How many points does the English League give a team for a victory, and how many for a tie? [13]
A. 1 for a win, 0 for a tie
B. 2 for a win, 1 for a tie
C. 3 for a win, 1 for a tie

7.33 What winner of three gold medals in three tries at the
      1988 Seoul Olympics also won the Sullivan Award in
      March, 1990, as America's outstanding amateur athlete?
      [18]
      A. Janet Evans
      B. Carl Lewis
      C. Steven Lewis

7.34 Who holds the American League record for playing in the
      most baseball games? [64]
      A. Ty Cobb
      B. Lou Gehrig
      C. Carl Yastrzemski

7.35 After finishing seventh, fifth, and third in her three
      previous tries, who won the Ladies World Figure Skating
      Championships in 1990? [25]
      A. Evelyn Grossman
      B. Midori Ito
      C. Jill Trenary

7.36 The complex African and Asian "pit-and-pebble" games,
      such as wari and omweso, are collectively known by
      what generic name? [8]
      A. mancala
      B. mandala
      C. mandela

7.37 Who set records as the youngest major league player both
      to lead a league in home runs and to hit 100 career home
      runs? [73]
      A. Hank Aaron
      B. Tony Conigliaro
      C. Mark McGwire

7.38 In 1990, Robert Gamez entered his first tournament as a
      professional, and won—in what sport? [47]
      A. figure skating
      B. golf
      C. tennis

7.39 Who is the only player ever to lead a league (or tie for the lead) in home runs for seven consecutive years? [34]
A. Harmon Killebrew
B. Ralph Kiner
C. Babe Ruth

7.40 After the yacht *Stars & Stripes* won the America's Cup race against New Zealand, a court ruled that *Stars & Stripes* had violated the rules of the competition. In what way? [41]
A. Some of its crew members were not U.S. citizens.
B. It was a catamaran instead of a single-hulled yacht.
C. It was designed with the aid of a computer.

7.41 The first time that the best computer chess machine in the world, "Deep Thought," played a two-game match with human world champion Gary Kasparov, was in 1989. What was the result? [71]
A. Deep Thought won both games.
B. There were two draws.
C. Kasparov won both games.

7.42 Tiger Stadium is the oldest ball park in the major leagues. When was it built? [2]
A. 1901
B. 1921
C. 1941

7.43 When Steve Largent retired from pro football in 1989, one of the many records he held was for catching the most touchdown passes in a career. How many did he catch? [37]
A. 50
B. 75
C. 100

7.44 Who, in 1990, became the first baseball player to sign a contract in which he would be paid more than $4 million a year? [46]
A. George Brett
B. Will Clark
C. Kirby Puckett

7.45 In what sport do U.S. and British/Irish amateurs compete against one another for the Walker Cup (men) and the Curtis Cup (women)? [75]
A. croquet
B. golf
C. tennis

7.46 Who set a record for most lifetime homers as a catcher, with 327? [55]
A. Johnny Bench
B. Yogi Berra
C. Carlton Fisk

7.47 Through the start of 1990, Herve Filonion had won more harness races than anyone else. Approximately how many? [24]
A. 120
B. 1,200
C. 12,000

7.48 During the 1980s, how many times did Yankee first baseman Don Mattingly start in the All-Star Game? [6]
A. 1
B. 5
C. 9

7.49 In a regular PGA Tour event, who shot a record 59 in one round at the Memphis Open in 1977? [51]
A. Al Geiberger
B. Jack Nicklaus
C. Tom Watson

7.50 In these three all-time sports records, which number is highest? [9]
A. the number of points scored by Kareem Abdul-Jabbar in his professional basketball career
B. the number of times Willie Shoemaker rode in a horse race
C. the number of yards Fran Tarkenton passed for as a pro quarterback

(3-Point Questions)

7.51 Who was the first woman athlete to win over $100,000 in a single season in any sport? [35]
   A. JoAnne Carner
   B. Chris Evert
   C. Billie Jean King
   D. Nancy Lopez

7.52 Who stole home the most times in his major league baseball career? [65]
   A. Lou Brock
   B. Max Carey
   C. Ty Cobb
   D. Jackie Robinson

7.53 In 1989, Javier Sotomayor of Cuba became first to successfully clear what height in a high jump competition? [16]
   A. 6 feet
   B. 7 feet
   C. 8 feet
   D. 9 feet

7.54 Which is not one of the three "suits" in a set of mah jongg tiles? [3]
   A. bamboos
   B. characters
   C. dots
   D. flowers

7.55 In Scrabble Crossword Game, the rarest, hardest-to-use letter tiles have a basic value of 10 points each. In the game's French edition, which of these is *not* a 10-point tile? [42]
   A. K
   B. Q
   C. W
   D. Y

7.56 Foxhall P. Keene was the first "10-goal rated player" in this sport in the U.S. What was the sport? [70]
  A. cricket
  B. ice hockey
  C. lacrosse
  D. polo

7.57 In Babe Ruth's major league debut in 1915, what happened? [22]
  A. He hit a game-winning home run for the New York Yankees.
  B. He made an error that cost his team the game.
  C. He pitched for the Boston Red Sox and won.
  D. He pitched for the New York Yankees and won.

7.58 Which of the following schools does *not* call its college football team the "Bulldogs"? [61]
  A. Cincinnati
  B. Georgia
  C. Mississippi State
  D. Yale

7.59 In the 1989 season, Joe Montana had the highest rating ever for a quarterback. Whose record did he break? [32]
  A. Sammy Baugh
  B. Dan Marino
  C. Joe Namath
  D. Milt Plum

7.60 Who was the first major league pitcher to throw three one-hitters in a space of four consecutive starts? [12]
  A. Steve Carlton
  B. Nolan Ryan
  C. Tom Seaver
  D. Dave Stieb

7.61 What college football team won the national
championship, based on the Associated Press poll of
sportswriters, the most often during the 1980s, including
the 1989-90 season? [45]
A. Alabama
B. Miami (of Florida)
C. Notre Dame
D. Penn State

7.62 In Japan, in what year were women first allowed to watch
a sumo wrestling match? [66]
A. 1778
B. 1878
C. 1978
D. never

7.63 Who holds the record for winning the most victories in a
row (11) on the professional golf tour? [28]
A. Byron Nelson
B. Jack Nicklaus
C. Ben Hogan
D. Arnold Palmer

7.64 Prior to Steffi Graf, who was the last woman to win the
Grand Slam of tennis—that is, to win the Australian
Open, the French Open, Wimbledon, and the U.S. Open
all in the same year? [39]
A. Margaret Court
B. Chris Evert
C. Billie Jean King
D. Martina Navratilova

7.65 In the 1980s, Louise Ann Bowles, a 50-year-old interior
designer from Honolulu, Hawaii, caught a Pacific blue
marlin that surpassed the women's world record on
80-pound-test line for this fish. Approximately how much
did the fish weigh? [23]
A. 95 pounds
B. 350 pounds
C. 950 pounds
D. 3,500 pounds

7.66 Which strategy board game, when bought new, comes with the most pieces? [54]
A. go
B. Polish checkers
C. reversi
D. xiang qi (Chinese chess)

7.67 Who was the first U.S. president to throw out a baseball at a baseball game? [11]
A. Grover Cleveland
B. Theodore Roosevelt
C. William Howard Taft
D. Harry Truman

7.68 What was the first coin-operated video game? [48]
A. Computer Space
B. Pac-Man
C. Pong
D. Space Invaders

7.69 During the decades of the 1970s and 1980s, only one major league baseball player hit 50 or more home runs in a season. Who? [31]
A. George Foster
B. Mark McGwire
C. Jim Rice
D. Willie Stargell

7.70 Which type of athlete would have trouble after (figuratively) "hitting the Wall"? [60]
A. a figure skater
B. an outfielder
C. a marathon runner
D. a pole vaulter

7.71 Through 1990, only one Division I-A college football team had over 700 wins. Which one? [5]
A. Alabama
B. Michigan
C. Notre Dame
D. Texas

7.72 Which of these four baseball stadiums has artificial grass? [67]
A. Candlestick Park
B. Comiskey Park
C. Riverfront Stadium
D. Shea Stadium

7.73 Which of these cities has twice served as host of the modern Winter Olympic Games? [38]
A. Innsbruck, Austria
B. Lake Placid, New York
C. St. Moritz, Switzerland
D. all of the above

7.74 Where did the Grey Cup trophy for the championship of Canadian football get its name? [52]
A. It was donated by a governor-general of Canada named Grey.
B. It was named for novelist Zane Grey.
C. It was named for the stadium where the game was first played.
D. The trophy itself is gray in color.

7.75 According to computer analysis, what is the most often landed on space in the game of Monopoly? [27]
A. Boardwalk
B. Go
C. Illinois Avenue
D. Reading Railroad

Chapter 8

Potpourri

Answers to questions in this chapter begin on page 186.

True or False?

(1-Point Questions)

8.1 The United States has issued both two-cent and three-cent coins. [12]

8.2 In a restaurant, dishes served "florentine" are prepared with broccoli. [51]

8.3 George Washington is known to have liked eating pineapples. [39]

8.4 The Taj Mahal (the one in India—not Donald Trump's Atlantic City casino) was built in the 17th century. [22]

8.5 No company listed on the New York Stock Exchange starts with the letter X. [69]

8.6 In population, Rio de Janeiro is the largest city in Brazil. [46]

8.7 A compact disk revolves at different speeds, slowing down as its edge is being read. [3]

8.8 In general, "prime" beef has a higher fat content than beef graded either "choice" or "select." [75]

8.9 The "O" in "OPEC" stands for "Oil." [32]

8.10 The Christmas plant known as holly is obtained from a variety of elm tree. [57]

8.11 The zodiac sign Sagittarius is represented by the Goat. [33]

8.12 Sleeping Beauty slept for 100 years before the handsome prince came to awaken her. [18]

8.13 The bore of a 16-gauge shotgun is larger than the bore of a 12-gauge shotgun. [41]

8.14 The average person in China eats more calories of food than the average person in the United States. [9]

8.15 *U.S. News & World Report* shortened its name to *U.S. News* in 1989. [61]

8.16 A "misogynist" is someone who hates children. [20]

8.17 For every man who is colorblind, there are about eight women who are colorblind. [49]

8.18 Snuff is a form of tobacco. [72]

8.19 Novelist John le Carré, noted for spy novels, was himself in the British Secret Service. [37]

8.20 Coffee was introduced to Europe from America. [67]

8.21 The Miller Brewing Company is owned by Philip Morris. [25]

8.22 Over the past generation in the U.S., the population's average IQ, as measured on standardized tests, has increased. [54]

8.23 The Stealth bomber is also known as the B-2. [34]

8.24 The line "These are the times that try men's souls" originated with Winston Churchill. [63]

8.25 In Esperanto, an "international language" invented by Dr. Ludwik Zamenhof and first presented to the public in 1887, all basic nouns end with the letter O. [27]

Multiple Choice

(2-Point Questions)

8.26 When did the Liberty Bell get its name? [55]
  A. when it was made, in 1701
  B. when it rang on July 4, 1776
  C. in the 19th century, when it became a symbol for the abolition of slavery

8.27 In the Roy Rogers-Dale Evans Museum in California, you will find both Roy's stuffed horse Trigger, and what horse of Dale's? [17]
  A. Buttermilk
  B. Daisy
  C. Scout

8.28 In law enforcement parlance, what is "smurfing"? [45]
  A. illegal dwarf-tossing
  B. laundering drug-money
  C. swindling a child

8.29 In 1989, a desk-bookcase made in Newport in the 1760s set a record auction price at auction for a piece of furniture. How much did it sell for? [6]
  A. $121,000
  B. $1,210,000
  C. $12,100,000

8.30 Whether or not he reached the North Pole in 1909 was long doubted by some, but a 1989 study suggests that he did after all. Who is he? [66]
  A. Roald Amundsen
  B. Robert E. Peary
  C. William Barents

8.31 When is China due to take over Hong Kong? [60]
  A. 1997
  B. 2000
  C. 2020

8.32 The Moon of Barods, a 24-carat diamond that Marilyn Monroe wore while singing "Diamonds Are a Girl's Best Friend" in the film *Gentlemen Prefer Blondes*, was auctioned off at Christie's for how much in 1990? [7]
  A. $97,000
  B. $297,000
  C. $497,000

8.33 What soft-drink company introduced the brand Slice? [74]
  A. Coca Cola
  B. Pepsico
  C. Seven Up

8.34 In what state does the smallest percentage of people live either in or within commuting distance of cities with populations of at least 50,000? [47]
  A. Alaska
  B. Idaho
  C. Vermont

8.35 Where did Malcolm Forbes hold a 70th birthday bash for
600 guests in 1989? [31]
  A. Calcutta, India
  B. Kuala Lumpur, Malaysia
  C. Tangier, Morocco

8.36 The NoRMA awards are given for excellence in what
field? [56]
  A. Broadway plays
  B. newspaper advertising
  C. TV reporting

8.37 What is the best grade of olive oil? [11]
  A. extra virgin
  B. pure virgin
  C. superfine virgin

8.38 Through January 1990, how many of the 10
highest-rated TV shows of all time were Super Bowls?
[36]
  A. 1
  B. 5
  C. 9

8.39 In which Soviet Republic do most people speak a
language that is identical to Romanian? [15]
  A. Armenia
  B. Latvia
  C. Moldavia

8.40 What kind of packaging, in some states, is required to
bear a triangle, a number, and the letters "PETE,"
"HDPE," "LDPE," "PP," or "PS"?[62]
  A. glass jars
  B. metal cans
  C. plastic bottles

8.41 In what decade were both Time Inc. and Warner
Brothers—which merged in 1989 to form the world's
largest media company—founded? [28]
  A. 1890s
  B. 1920s
  C. 1950s

8.42 In the phrase "six- to eight-foot waves," what kind of hyphenation is used? [8]
    A. sequential hyphenation
    B. successive hyphenation
    C. suspensive hyphenation

8.43 In the U.S., about how many people mail their income tax returns on the last possible day? [73]
    A. one quarter
    B. one third
    C. one half

8.44 When did the Philadelphia mint start putting a "P" mint mark on quarters? [30]
    A. 1960
    B. 1980
    C. never

8.45 On which of these calendars is the current year the highest? [59]
    A. Chinese lunar calendar
    B. Gregorian calendar
    C. Jewish calendar

8.46 In the 1988 elections, which Political Action Committee gave the most money to federal candidates? [21]
    A. Association of Trial Lawyers of America
    B. International Brotherhood of Teamsters
    C. National Association of Realtors

8.47 Who said, "The best way to resist temptation is to yield to it." [52]
    A. Lord Byron
    B. Omar Khayyam
    C. Oscar Wilde

8.48 What is Simplesse, NutraSweet's fat substitute, made of? [2]
    A. a blend of proteins from egg white and milk
    B. fat molecules altered to be too large to digest
    C. molecules that are the mirror-image of normal fat molecules

8.49 Which item was owned by the fewest U.S. households in
1990? [68]
  A. compact disk player
  B. cordless telephone
  C. home computer

8.50 As of 1990, what country's population had the lowest
fertility rate (fewest children per adult female) in the
world? [14]
  A. Italy
  B. Sweden
  C. United States

(3-Point Questions)

8.51 Which of these vegetables is *not* used to make V-8 juice?
[42]
  A. beet
  B. cabbage
  C. carrot
  D. spinach

8.52 What is the most frequently used noun in the English
language? [4]
  A. car
  B. people
  C. time
  D. way

8.53 The most-used denomination of U.S. currency is the $1
bill. What bill is used second most? [64]
  A. $5
  B. $10
  C. $20
  D. $100

8.54 What were the most popular first names given to boy and
girl babies in the U.S. in the year 1900? [35]
  A. George and Anne
  B. John and Mary
  C. Joseph and Catherine
  D. William and Elizabeth

8.55 Where did Lenox china originate? [50]
  A. London, England
  B. New England
  C. New Jersey
  D. the Isle of Jersey

8.56 Which of the following is one of the British names for the arrangement of stars that Americans call "the Big Dipper"? [24]
  A. the Big Dog
  B. the Dragon
  C. the Hat
  D. the Plow

8.57 When completed in 2005, the Fresh Kills Garbage Pyramid on Staten Island, New York, will be taller and heavier than the Great Pyramid of Cheops. How much will the Garbage Pyramid weigh? [58]
  A. 500,000 tons
  B. 5 million tons
  C. 50 million tons
  D. 500 million tons

8.58 Who enters the annual Van Cliburn International Competition? [29]
  A. chefs
  B. chess players
  C. pianists
  D. squash players

8.59 Whose first spoken words on film were "Give me a whiskey, ginger ale on the side—and don't be stingy, baby"? [48]
  A. Lauren Bacall
  B. Humphey Bogart
  C. W.C. Fields
  D. Greta Garbo

8.60 What is the official two-letter postal abbreviation for
Alaska? [19]
   A. AA
   B. AL
   C. AK
   D. AS

8.61 What cover story gave both *Time* and *Newsweek* their
best-selling covers of the 1980s? [71]
   A. the eruption of Mt. St. Helens
   B. the Falklands war
   C. the first Reagan-Gorbachev summit meeting
   D. John Lennon's death

8.62 According to a late 1980s *Beverage Media* poll of 400
bartenders, what is the favorite drink of male customers?
[10]
   A. beer
   B. bourbon
   C. scotch
   D. vodka

8.63 According to a late 1980s *Beverage Media* poll of 400
bartenders, what is the favorite drink of female
customers? [40]
   A. beer
   B. margarita
   C. peach schnapps and orange juice
   D. white wine

8.64 The name of Florida's capital, Tallahassee, comes from
two Creek Indian words meaning what? [1]
   A. big meadow
   B. old town
   C. red flowers
   D. sunny place

8.65 Which member of the Ivy League was founded under the
name "King's College"? [44]
   A. Brown
   B. Columbia
   C. Cornell
   D. Dartmouth

8.66 These four Australian terms can all be found in the lyrics of the song "Waltzing Matilda." Which one is a tree? [53]
A. billabong
B. coolibah
C. jumbuck
D. tucker-bag

8.67 Among his other accomplishments, Joe Namath will always be remembered for demonstrating the product in a pantyhose commercial. But what brand of pantyhose was Joe wearing? [23]
A. Beautymist
B. Hanes
C. No Nonsense
D. Silky Soft

8.68 What TV talk-show host, in 1988, had a house torn down that he had bought just a few months earlier for $6.8 million? [38]
A. Johnny Carson
B. Phil Donahue
C. Jay Leno
D. David Letterman

8.69 Candlemas, a name for the feast of the Purification, has also become known as what day in the U.S.? [70]
A. April Fool's Day
B. Groundhog Day
C. Halloween
D. Thanksgiving

8.70 In England, Guy Fawkes Day is named for one of the Gunpowder Plot conspirators who tried to kill what ruler, along with the members of Parliament, in 1605? [13]
A. Charles I
B. Elizabeth I
C. Henry VIII
D. James I

8.71 Reginald Kenneth Dwight is better known as who? [26]
   A. Johnny Carson
   B. Reggie Jackson
   C. Elton John
   D. Tom Hanks

8.72 What was the name of the mythical lake in which King Arthur was said to have received his sword, and where later he supposedly died? [65]
   A. Avalon
   B. Camelot
   C. Shalimar
   D. Ventura

8.73 Birnbaum, Fielding, Fodor, and Frommer are all names of series of books on what subject? [43]
   A. cooking
   B. computers
   C. nature
   D. travel

8.74 When did cigarette commercials disappear from television? [5]
   A. 1966
   B. 1971
   C. 1976
   D. 1981

8.75 Which of the following did *not* take place in the year 1900? [16]
   A. the first Barnum & Bailey's circus
   B. the first College Board Scholastic Aptitude tests
   C. the first launching of a rigid airship by Ferdinand von Zeppelin
   D. the first Davis Cup tennis match between the U.S. and Great Britain

Chapter 9

1-Point Questions

Answers to questions in this chapter begin on page 188.

True or False?

9.1 Conductors on Amtrak trains accept major credit cards for the payment of fares. [18]

9.2 Dr. Joyce Brothers won over $100,000 as a game show contestant in the mid-1950s. [57]

9.3 Allspice is a blend of cinnamon, nutmeg, and cloves. [31]

9.4 Barbra Streisand was never a member of her high school glee club. [10]

9.5 Babe Ruth was the first player ever to hit a home run in an All-Star Game. [69]

9.6 The salary of the president of the United States is exempt from federal income tax. [46]

9.7 Prior to *On Golden Pond*, Henry Fonda and his daughter Jane never appeared in a movie together. [82]

9.8 Twelvepenny nails are so called because there was a time at which they cost twelvepence a hundred. [36]

9.9 Oklahoma City is the only state capital whose name contains the name of it state. [60]

9.10 The lima bean is named for the city of Lima, Peru. [21]

9.11 The man who delivered the eulogy describing George Washington as "first in war, first in peace, first in the hearts of his countrymen" was Robert E. Lee's father. [3]

9.12 Jay Silverheels, who played Tonto on the TV series *The Lone Ranger*, was actually the son of a Mohawk chief. [75]

9.13 Soybean oil is the most widely used vegetable oil in the world. [40]

9.14 Anne Frank, the young girl who was the author of a famous diary, and her sister Margot sent letters to two pen pals in Iowa in 1940. [64]

9.15 The dog Spuds MacKenzie acts as the mascot for Miller Lite beer. [24]

9.16 There are no United Nations members whose names, in English, begin with the letter Q. [70]

9.17 One thousand is one thousand percent of one hundred. [13]

9.18 The father of former Indian Prime Minister Indira was Mohandas K. (Mahatma) Gandhi. [87]

9.19 The stock market usually goes up in years in which the NFC team wins the Super Bowl, and down when the AFC team wins. [44]

9.20 A male and a female swan are known respectively as a "cob" and a "pen."[66]

9.21 The value of all the $1 bills in circulation is greater than the value of all the $5 bills in circulation. [37]

9.22 Natalie Wood's first film appearance was as a child in *Miracle on 34th Street*. [22]

9.23 When the National Hockey League was formed in 1917, only teams representing Canadian cities were included. [68]

9.24 The cover price of the debut issue of *Life* magazine, on November 23, 1936, was 10 cents. [33]

9.25 As written here, the word "accordian" is spelled correctly. [84]

9.26 If New York's Governor Mario Cuomo had been chosen by the Democrats to run for President in 1988, he would have been the first Italian-American member of a major-party ticket. [15]

9.27 The Adidas Corporation took its name from its founder, Adi Dassler. [92]

9.28 Fess Parker not only played Davy Crockett, he also sang the Top-10 1955 hit "Ballad of Davy Crockett." [2]

9.29 Art Carney was once a "big band" singer. [77]

9.30 Louis Brandeis was the first Jewish Supreme Court chief justice. [28]

9.31 "Perestroika" is a Russian word that means "openness," and which summarizes Mikhail Gorbachev's strategy for change in the Soviet Union. [9]

9.32 With a pair of properly weighted, standard dice, there is one chance in six of throwing a total of seven. [88]

9.33 Through 1990, no "wild card" team ever won the Super Bowl. [50]

9.34 Hiawatha was a beautiful Indian Girl. [98]

9.35 "Old Ironsides" was a nickname given to Andrew Jackson during the War of 1812. [61]

9.36 A peck is larger than a bushel. [27]

9.37 Michelangelo created the classic Renaissance painting *The Last Supper*. [91]

9.38 At the 1988 Reagan-Gorbachev summit, the U.S. finally recognized the 1940 annexation of Latvia by the Soviet Union. [42]

9.39 Termites and white ants are in fact the same insects. [83]

9.40 No World Series has ever been played in which every game was won by shutout. [11]

9.41 There are fewer than half a million seconds in a week. [47]

9.42 In the poem that begins "I shot an arrow into the air/It fell to earth, I know not where," the arrow is never found. [25]

9.43 A string quartet employs four musicians, but only three kinds of instruments. [100]

9.44 If a pilot says "Roger," it means "over and out." [53]

9.45 According to the International Association of Ice Cream Manufacturers, the average New Englander eats more ice cream than the average Southerner. [1]

9.46 Though they were the Federation's foes in *Star Trek*, the Klingons are now its allies in *Star Trek: The Next Generation*. [14]

9.47 Bette Midler had her first baby at age 40. [76]

9.48 Being married to two persons at once is "bigamy," and being married to three persons at once is called "trigamy." [30]

9.49 Soccer originated in the United States. [73]

9.50 In Spanish, the adjective *esposado* can mean either "newly married" or "handcuffed." [96]

9.51 USX Corporation is the largest steel producer in the United States. [54]

9.52 The Disney feature film *Cinderella* has grossed more money at the box office than the film *Snow White and the Seven Dwarfs*. [79]

9.53 Beverly Hills, California, is named for the Boston suburb of Beverly, Massachusetts. [12]

9.54 At a racetrack, the "exacta" and the "perfecta" are the same thing. [86]

9.55 No Alfred Hitchcock film ever won the Academy Award for best picture. [97]

9.56 According to a study at the Stanford Center for Research in Disease Prevention, a person tends to gain more weight from eating a calorie of fat than from eating a calorie of nonfat. [39]

9.57 In the opera *The Barber of Seville*, the barber's name is Rigoletto. [89]

9.58 The star in the upper left corner of a United States flag symbolizes the state of Delaware, which was the first state to ratify the Constitution. [71]

9.59 Woodpeckers can locate insect larvae by hearing them. [4]

9.60 Elvis Presley had more consecutive singles reach the top five on the *Billboard* charts than the Beatles. [49]

9.61 When the notorious Lizzie Borden was tried for murder, she was found guilty and executed. [32]

9.62 Besides appearing in *Poltergeist*, Heather O'Rourke also played Ashley Pfister's daughter on the TV sitcom *Happy Days*. [6]

9.63 According to a 1989 Baylor University study, football players who breathe oxygen on the sidelines recover from muscle fatigue almost twice as fast as those who just breathe the air. [56]

9.64 "Marmalade" comes from a word that means "orange." [99]

9.65 "Vertigo" is another name for the fear of heights. [43]

9.66 Despite its name, scientists have no evidence that there is milk anywhere in the Milky Way. [90]

9.67 The TV cliché, "Will the real John Doe please stand up?" came from the game show *I've Got a Secret*. [62]

9.68 One of the main characters in Oscar Wilde's *The Importance of Being Earnest* is someone named Ernest. [26]

9.69 Science-fiction writer Isaac Asimov was born in Russia. [55]

9.70 Supreme Court Justice Sandra Day O'Connor's maiden name is O'Connor. [93]

9.71 A person who goes to a "normal" school graduates with a degree in psychology. [72]

9.72 Most of the Susan B. Anthony dollars that were minted from 1979 to 1981 never entered circulation, and are still being stored by the U.S. Mint. [41]

9.73 Congress now requires all beverage cans manufactured in the United States to be made of aluminum. [59]

9.74 The musical *A Little Night Music* is based on a movie by Ingmar Bergman. [80]

9.75 Kodak was forced to leave the instant photography business after losing a patent infringement lawsuit to Polaroid in 1985. [19]

9.76 U.S. surveyors and mapmakers use the U.S. Survey foot instead of the international foot, even though the U.S. Survey foot is slightly longer. [35]

9.77 To a stamp collector, "E.F.O.s" are stamps bearing overprints in both English and French. [78]

9.78 In England, the term "napkin" is used only to refer to paper napkins. [51]

9.79 Felix Unger was the overly fussy half of *The Odd Couple*. [95]

9.80 Michael Dukakis's father was the first Greek immigrant to graduate from Harvard Medical School. [8]

9.81 Actress Alessandra Mussolini is both Benito Mussolini's granddaughter and Sophia Loren's niece. [16]

9.82 Anna Freud, who became one of the world's leading psychoanalysts, was the oldest of Sigmund Freud's children. [81]

9.83 The first opera by an American-born composer to be performed at La Scala was *Porgy and Bess*. [38]

9.84 After years of struggling with the rumor that its
man-in-the-moon logo was linked to Satanic worship,
Procter & Gamble changed its logo to a simple "P&G."
[94]

9.85 There are no longer any Playboy clubs in the United
States. [48]

9.86 In 1988, an unpublished Sherlock Holmes manuscript by
Sir Arthur Conan Doyle was discovered, titled "The Five
Orange Pips." [23]

9.87 In the United States, more artificial sweeteners are used
in sodas than in all dried foods combined. [5]

9.88 *Bonanza* was the first TV western series to present
90-minute telecasts. [67]

9.89 Next to Asia, Africa is the most populous continent. [45]

9.90 Raymond Chandler is the author of the *Spenser* mystery
novel series. [74]

9.91 The 1938 film *The Adventures of Robin Hood* was
originally shot in color. [34]

9.92 *The Raw and The Cooked* is the name of an album by the
group Fine Young Cannibals. [20]

9.93 One tablespoon is exactly equal to three teaspoons. [65]

9.94 No song title beginning with the letter X was in the Top
10 in the 1960s, '70s, or '80s. [7]

9.95 A statute mile, equal to 5,280 feet, is longer than a
nautical mile. [52]

9.96 The number that Americans call a trillion is called a
billion by the British. [85]

9.97 It is possible for a bill that Congress passes to become law even though the president neither signs nor vetoes it. [29]

9.98 Richard Harris's recording of "MacArthur Park" reached number one in the charts, but Donna Summer's version of the song did not. [58]

9.99 Of the Seven Wonders of the Ancient World listed in *The World Almanac*, only the Egyptian pyramids remain to this day. [17]

9.100 Only female mosquitoes bite. [63]

Chapter 10

2-Point Questions

Answers to questions in this chapter begin on page 191.

10.1 Approximately when was the wheel invented? [29]
A. 5500 B.C.
B. 3500 B.C.
C. 1500 B.C.

10.2 Which of these comedies was the top-rated TV show for five consecutive years? [5]
A. *All in the Family*
B. *I Love Lucy*
C. *The Beverly Hillbillies*

10.3 On sound recordings, a copyright notice should begin with what letter inside a circle? [78]
A. C
B. P
C. R

10.4 According to *Billboard* charts, who was the first artist in the rock era to have four Top-10 singles from a debut album? [62]
A. Whitney Houston
B. Cyndi Lauper
C. Madonna

10.5 The Amtrak service known as the Coast Starlight runs between what two cities? [89]
A. Los Angeles and Seattle
B. Miami and New York
C. New Orleans and San Antonio

10.6 In what adventure story would you meet the crafty pirate Long John Silver? [30]
A. *Captains Courageous*
B. *Kidnapped*
C. *Treasure Island*

10.7 During a regulation round, a golfer is permitted to use an assortment of no more than how many clubs? [42]
A. 10
B. 14
C. any number that will fit into a standard golf bag

10.8 The line "All is for the best in the best of all possible worlds" is from what? [92]
A. Beckett's *Waiting for Godot*
B. Shakespeare's *The Merchant of Venice*
C. Voltaire's *Candide*

10.9 In the nursery rhyme that begins, "Rub-a-dub-dub/Three men in a tub," who are the men? [13]
A. Solomon Grundy's children
B. the butcher, the baker, the candlestick maker
C. three men of Gotham

10.10 Which amendment to the Constitution protects citizens against "unreasonable searches and seizures"? [82]
A. the first
B. the fourth
C. the fourteenth

10.11 What American composer of popular music also wrote an opera titled *Treemonisha*? [58]
A. Irving Berlin
B. Scott Joplin
C. Richard Rogers

10.12 Which U.S. city hosted two World's Fairs this century, both at Flushing Meadows-Corona Park? [67]
  A. Chicago
  B. New Orleans
  C. New York City

10.13 Which of these major Academy Awards did *Gone With the Wind* not win? [51]
  A. best actor
  B. best actress
  C. best picture

10.14 Where was George Bush born? [26]
  A. Maine
  B. Massachusetts
  C. Texas

10.15 From whom did Europeans first learn about chocolate? [71]
  A. Africans
  B. Aztecs
  C. East Indians

10.16 In 1983, after holding the America's Cup for 125 years, the New York Yacht Club lost it to what country? [91]
  A. Australia
  B. France
  C. New Zealand

10.17 Which musical comedy featured the songs "The Party's Over" and "Just in Time"? [2]
  A. *Bells Are Ringing*
  B. *The King and I*
  C. *My Fair Lady*

10.18 When was the Palace of Governors built in Santa Fe, New Mexico? [76]
  A. 1610
  B. 1710
  C. 1810

10.19 What was the Hunchback of Notre Dame's real name?
[87]
A. Jean Valjean
B. Quasimodo
C. Vincent

10.20 Who wrote the words, "Indeed I tremble for my country
when I reflect that God is just"? [36]
A. Simon Bolivar
B. George Bernard Shaw
C. Thomas Jefferson

10.21 Cartoonist Al Hirshfeld began hiding the name "Nina" in
his cartoons for *The New York Times* in 1945. He chose
the name Nina because it is also whose name? [63]
A. his daughter's
B. his mother's
C. his wife's

10.22 In basketball, what is a referee indicating when he forms
the letter "T" with his hands? [8]
A. technical foul
B. time out
C. traveling

10.23 Of the years 2000, 2050, and 2100, how many will be
leap years? [74]
A. 0
B. 1
C. 2

10.24 Which TV comedy couple, in real life, were born on the
very same day and year? [93]
A. Carroll O'Connor and Jean Stapleton of *All in the
Family*
B. Max Wright and Ann Schedeen of *Alf*
C. Michael Gross and Meredith Baxter of *Family Ties*

10.25 Which of the following is spelled correctly? [49]
A. milennium
B. millenium
C. millennium

10.26 What major league pitcher had lost the fewest games by
the time he won 100? [96]
   A. Bob Feller
   B. Whitey Ford
   C. Dwight Gooden

10.27 In the book *Lost Horizon*, where was the fictional city of
Shangri-La? [11]
   A. an island in the South Pacific
   B. the jungles of Africa
   C. the mountains of Tibet

10.28 What did "Weird Al" Yankovic call his album that
contained a parody of a song from Michael Jackson's
album *Bad*? [28]
   A. *Badder*
   B. *Even Worse*
   C. *Good*

10.29 In 1988 and 1989, who became the first golfer since Ben
Hogan in 1950 and 1951 to win two consecutive U.S.
Opens? [66]
   A. Seve Ballesteros
   B. Greg Norman
   C. Curtis Strange

10.30 In what year did Wyatt Earp die? [21]
   A. 1889
   B. 1909
   C. 1929

10.31 Which philosopher believed that "whatever is rational is
real and whatever is real is rational"? [45]
   A. Georg Hegel
   B. Sören Kierkegaard
   C. Jean-Paul Sartre

10.32 In what state did Red Grange, the "Galloping Ghost,"
play both college and professional football? [95]
   A. Illinois
   B. New York
   C. Ohio

10.33 From 1980 to 1990, in the U.S., which age group had the highest percentage increase in population? [17]
  A. 5- to 9-year-olds
  B. 55- to 59-year-olds
  C. 95- to 99-year-olds

10.34 Among names of U.S. states, what is the most common first letter? [55]
  A. A
  B. M
  C. N

10.35 At one point in his career, middleweight boxer Sugar Ray Robinson had a record of 128 wins and only one loss. To whom was the loss? [4]
  A. Rocky Graziano
  B. Jake LaMotta
  C. Tony Zale

10.36 "Room temperature" is 68 degrees Fahrenheit. What is the equivalent temperature in degrees Celsius? [73]
  A. 20
  B. 30
  C. 40

10.37 During his eight years in office, how many summit conferences did Ronald Reagan have with Mikhail Gorbachev? [83]
  A. 2
  B. 5
  C. 8

10.38 The TV series *The Days and Nights of Molly Dodd* moved from NBC to what cable network? [77]
  A. The Disney Channel
  B. Lifetime
  C. Showtime

10.39 The annual Outland Trophy is awarded to what collegiate athlete? [44]
  A. the best all-around athlete in track and field
  B. the outstanding interior lineman in football
  C. the outstanding female basketball player

10.40 What jazz singer was known as the "Divine One"? [60]
  A. Ella Fitzgerald
  B. Billie Holiday
  C. Sarah Vaughan

10.41 At common law, which interest in land would give its owner the greatest rights? [20]
  A. fee simple
  B. fee tail
  C. life estate

10.42 About how much beer does the average person in the United States drink each year? [72]
  A. 24 pints
  B. 24 quarts
  C. 24 gallons

10.43 Fur trader Solomon Juneau helped found, and was the first mayor of, what city? [32]
  A. Juneau, Alaska
  B. Milwaukee, Wisconsin
  C. Montreal, Canada

10.44 What religion's tenets are set forth in a collection of works known as the *Veda*? [16]
  A. Buddism
  B. Hinduism
  C. Taoism

10.45 More often than not, the major-league baseball All-Star Game has been played in which month? [54]
  A. June
  B. July
  C. August

10.46 In winning his record 20 major golf titles, which event did Jack Nicklaus win the most times? [9]
  A. the British Open
  B. the Masters
  C. the U.S. Open

10.47 In the process of testing new drugs before they are
approved for general use, what are "pre-clinical trials"?
[47]
A. tests by computer simulation of molecular interactions
B. tests on animals
C. tests on humans

10.48 What is the Latin word for the number "six"? [37]
A. hex
B. sex
C. six

10.49 What is the name of the trick in which a yo-yo is thrown
down and stays down? [3]
A. rocking the boat
B. sleeping
C. walking the dog

10.50 Who wrote the line, "A Jug of Wine, a Loaf of
Bread—and Thou"? [18]
A. Elizabeth Barrett Browning
B. Edward Fitzgerald
C. William Wordsworth

10.51 The annual Wimbledon tennis tournament is played on
what kind of surface? [34]
A. asphalt
B. clay
C. grass

10.52 Who in American films was known as "the Great
Profile"? [81]
A. John Barrymore
B. Errol Flynn
C. Marilyn Monroe

10.53 In Edgar Rice Burroughs's *At the Earth's Core* and other
novels, what is the name of the underground continent
500 miles beneath the earth's surface? [41]
A. Morlock
B. Ozymandia
C. Pellucidar

10.54 In 1959, baseball's Most Valuable Player awards in both
major leagues went to players who played for teams from
the same city. What was the city? [6]
A. Chicago
B. New York
C. St. Louis

10.55 Who wrote the poem beginning "Life is real! Life is
earnest!"? [79]
A. Henry Wadsworth Longfellow
B. Walt Whitman
C. William Wordsworth

10.56 In the movie *Tootsie*, Dustin Hoffman portrayed a man
who posed as a woman in order to find work. What was
this character's profession? [25]
A. actor
B. clothing-store clerk
C. doctor

10.57 On August 3, 1989, in the first inning of a game against
the Houston Astros, the Cincinnati Reds set a modern
record for most hits in an inning. How many did they get?
[88]
A. 12
B. 16
C. 20

10.58 What musical comedy featured the songs "A Lot of Livin'
To Do" and "Put on a Happy Face"? [22]
A. *Bye Bye Birdie*
B. *Oklahoma!*
C. *Wonderful Town*

10.59 Which of these sluggers never won a league home run
title? [75]
A. Ernie Banks
B. Stan Musial
C. Darryl Strawberry

10.60 Who starred opposite Ethel Merman in the original Broadway production of *Gypsy*? [57]
   A. Jack Klugman
   B. Karl Malden
   C. Robert Preston

10.61 In what city was the fictitious St. Gregory Hotel located on the TV series *Hotel*? [65]
   A. Boston
   B. New York
   C. San Francisco

10.62 In what country does the average person buy the most flowers per year? [38]
   A. Japan
   B. the Netherlands
   C. United States

10.63 Which product appeared on the market first? [59]
   A. Hallmark Cards
   B. Lincoln Logs
   C. Maidenform Bras

10.64 If someone wants to have a tête-à-tête with you, what do they want to do? [12]
   A. dance
   B. kiss
   C. talk

10.65 What is the Paris subway system called? [56]
   A. le métro
   B. le sous-terrain
   C. le subway

10.66 When the Denver Broncos lost their fourth Super Bowl in January, 1990, what team did they tie for the most Super Bowl losses? [100]
   A. Dallas Cowboys
   B. Miami Dolphins
   C. Minnesota Vikings

10.67 By most accounts, what was first sold at the 1904 St.
Louis World's Fair? [68]
  A. Belgian waffles
  B. chewing gum
  C. ice cream cones

10.68 When Michael Jackson became the lead singer of the
Jackson Five, how old was he? [50]
  A. 5
  B. 10
  C. 15

10.69 Who played two pairs of twins in the 1988 comedy film
Big Business? [31]
  A. Shelley Long and Bette Midler
  B. Bette Midler and Lily Tomlin
  C. Lily Tomlin and Shelley Long

10.70 When was TV personality Dick Clark's 50th birthday?
[40]
  A. 1979
  B. 1984
  C. 1989

10.71 *Mister Rogers' Neighborhood* is a long-running PBS
series. What is Mister Rogers's first name? [7]
  A. Ed
  B. Fred
  C. Ted

10.72 In swimming, which kind of stroke produces the fastest
world record times in both 100-meter and 200-meter
races? [94]
  A. backstroke
  B. breaststroke
  C. butterfly

10.73 What kind of dog was the film star Rin Tin Tin? [80]
  A. a collie
  B. a German shepherd
  C. a Husky

10.74 *Nora, The Real Life of Molly Bloom,* is the biography of
Nora Barnacle, who was the wife of what writer? [99]
  A. James Joyce
  B. Eugene O'Neill
  C. Tennessee Williams

10.75 In what country was pop singer Sade born? [86]
  A. Nigeria
  B. Sudan
  C. United Kingdom

10.76 What actor's character traded places with Eddie
Murphy's character in the film *Trading Places*? [53]
  A. Dan Ackroyd
  B. John Candy
  C. Nick Nolte

10.77 What is the English translation of the opera title *Die
Fliedermaus*? [33]
  A. The Bat
  B. The Cat
  C. The Rat

10.78 What Flemish, Baroque artist painted *The Garden of Love*
in the 1630s? [64]
  A. Rembrandt
  B. Rubens
  C. van Dyck

10.79 According to Mother Goose, how many fiddlers did Old
King Cole have? [10]
  A. 3
  B. 12
  C. 24

10.80 The krona, krone, and kroner are the currencies of what
three countries, respectively? [98]
  A. Bulgaria, Yugoslavia, Romania
  B. Iceland, Netherlands, Belgium
  C. Sweden, Denmark, Norway

10.81 Who wrote *The Book of Mormon*? [52]
   A. William Miller
   B. Joseph Smith
   C. Brigham Young

10.82 Who won Pulitzer Prizes in both 1987 and 1990 for the dramas *Fences* and *The Piano Lesson*? [43]
   A. Sam Shepard
   B. Alfred Uhry
   C. August Wilson

10.83 Which of these African colonies was the first to become independent? [19]
   A. Angola
   B. Nigeria
   C. Sudan

10.84 What does the Spanish word mañana mean? [48]
   A. today
   B. tomorrow
   C. yesterday

10.85 Who was the Greek god of love? [1]
   A. Cupid
   B. Eros
   C. Pan

10.86 In 1989, the spaceship *Voyager2* found geysers on Triton, a moon of which planet? [97]
   A. Saturn
   B. Uranus
   C. Neptune

10.87 If you take out a mortgage from a bank in order to buy a house from someone, who is the mortgagee? [61]
   A. the bank
   B. the seller of the house
   C. you

10.88 When *The Tonight Show* debuted (as *Tonight*) in 1954, who was its host? [84]
A. Steve Allen
B. Johnny Carson
C. Jack Paar

10.89 In 1987, Don Mattingly set a record for hitting home runs in the most consecutive games. In how many games in a row did he hit at least one home run? [24]
A. 4
B. 8
C. 12

10.90 Who directed the movie flop *Ishtar*? [69]
A. Blake Edwards
B. Elaine May
C. Oliver Stone

10.91 In 1990, Pepsico completed the largest deal ever between a U.S. company and the Soviet Union. In return for Pepsi-Cola, what did Pepsico *not* get? [85]
A. furs
B. ships
C. vodka

10.92 Which of these teams has never won two consecutive Superbowls? [23]
A. Dallas Cowboys
B. Miami Dolphins
C. Pittsburgh Steelers

10.93 Tempo and Festiva are both made by what car manufacturer? [35]
A. Chrysler
B. Ford
C. General Motors

10.94 From the time of Maximilian until the 1930s, when it became a museum, Chapultepec Castle was the traditional home of what country's leaders? [90]
A. Austria
B. Spain
C. Mexico

10.95 Robinson Crusoe Island is one of the Juan Fernandez
Islands, which are located where? [39]
A. in the Atlantic, off the coast of West Africa
B. in the Indian Ocean, off the coast of East Africa
C. in the Pacific, off the coast of Chile

10.96 For what film did Julie Andrews win the Academy Award
for best actress? [14]
A. *Mary Poppins*
B. *The Sound of Music*
C. *Victor/Victoria*

10.97 What toy company makes G.I. Joe action figures? [27]
A. Hasbro
B. Mattel
C. Milton Bradley

10.98 What baseball award did Jerome Walton win in 1989?
[15]
A. American League Manager of the Year
B. National League Rookie of the Year
C. Most Valuable Player of the World Series

10.99 Which country does Vietnam *not* border? [70]
A. Cambodia
B. Laos
C. Thailand

10.100 A 1,700-foot subway tunnel, which was sealed up in 1861
due to financing problems, was rediscovered in 1979 in
nearly perfect condition. In what city is it located? [46]
A. Boston
B. New York City
C. Philadelphia

Chapter 11

3-Point Questions

Answers to questions in this chapter begin on page 194.

11.1 When the Brownie Box Camera was introduced by
Eastman Kodak in 1900, what was its retail price? [66]
A. $1
B. $10
C. $100
D. $1,000

11.2 What play, when it closed in 1990, had been performed
on Broadway the most times? [44]
A.· *Annie*
B. *A Chorus Line*
C. *Fiddler on the Roof*
D. *Hello Dolly*

11.3 "What you do not want done to yourself, do not do to
others" is a variation on the Golden Rule that is attributed
to what pre-Christian thinker? [87]
A. Buddha
B. Confucius
C. Plato
D. Zoroaster

11.4 Which of these is *not* the title of a book by Dr. Seuss? [13]
    A. *The Cat in the Hat*
    B. *The Frog in the Bog*
    C. *Hop on Pop*
    D. *Hunches in Bunches*

11.5 Which of the following composers did *not* complete exactly nine symphonies? [101]
    A. Beethoven
    B. Bruckner
    C. Dvořák
    D. Haydn

11.6 The British royal family, now known as the House of Windsor, changed its name from what in response to anti-German feeling at the outbreak of World War I? [24]
    A. Hanover
    B. Hapsburg
    C. Hohenzollern
    D. Saxe-Coburg

11.7 Which of these oils is the highest in polyunsaturates and the lowest in saturated fat of any commercial oil? [64]
    A. coconut oil
    B. corn oil
    C. olive oil
    D. safflower oil

11.8 To whom did Robert Herrick dedicate his poem that begins, "Gather ye rosebuds while ye may"? [40]
    A. farmers
    B. his wife
    C. the king of England
    D. virgins

11.9 Who was Hannibal Hamlin? [75]
    A. a character in Mark Twain's *The Adventures of Huckleberry Finn*
    B. a character on the TV series *The A Team*
    C. a vice president under Abraham Lincoln
    D. the "Pied Piper" of a children's story

11.10 Approximately what percentage of Canadians live within
150 miles of the United States? [3]
    A. 15%
    B. 35%
    C. 55%
    D. 75%

11.11 In December, 1986, billionaire H. Ross Perot was ousted
from what company's board of directors for criticizing
the company's chairman? [21]
    A. General Dynamics
    B. General Electric
    C. General Mills
    D. General Motors

11.12 Who played the title role in the original Broadway
production of *The Unsinkable Molly Brown*? [60]
    A. Barbara Cook
    B. Tammy Grimes
    C. Angela Lansbury
    D. Debbie Reynolds

11.13 When did the Statue of Liberty celebrate its 100th
anniversary? [36]
    A. 1976
    B. 1986
    C. 1987
    D. 1988

11.14 When, if ever, were cable shows first allowed to compete
against regular broadcast TV shows in the Emmy
Awards? [82]
    A. 1980
    B. 1988
    C. They have always been allowed to.
    D. They have never been allowed to.

11.15 What did the average shopper pay for a pound of coffee
in 1940? [46]
    A. 10 cents
    B. 25 cents
    C. 50 cents
    D. 1 dollar

11.16 Which writer of the New Testament is called "beloved physician"? [69]
   A. Matthew
   B. Mark
   C. Luke
   D. John

11.17 Which of the following states has more than one seat in the House of Representatives? [10]
   A. Alaska
   B. Hawaii
   C. Vermont
   D. Wyoming

11.18 Which of these performers did *not* contribute her voice to 1987's successful album *Trio*? [31]
   A. Emmylou Harris
   B. Reba McEntire
   C. Dolly Parton
   D. Linda Ronstadt

11.19 Which member of the Watergate family gave us the 1978 bestseller *The Ends of Power*? [57]
   A. John Dean
   B. John Ehrlichman
   C. H.R. Haldeman
   D. Gordon Liddy

11.20 What musical comedy with a Cole Porter score was based on the Greta Garbo film comedy *Ninotchka*? [18]
   A. *Anything Goes*
   B. *Can Can*
   C. *Flora, the Red Menace*
   D. *Silk Stockings*

11.21 Jackie Presser, the late Teamster President, was the nation's highest-paid union boss in 1984. How much did he earn from the Teamsters that year? [70]
   A. $107,500
   B. $215,000
   C. $530,000
   D. $1,060,000

11.22 The fictional city of Arkham found in certain H.P.
Lovecraft works is supposed to be located in what real
U.S. state? [63]
A. Colorado
B. Florida
C. Massachusetts
D. New York

11.23 Which of these Supreme Court justices was *not*
nominated by Ronald Reagan? [17]
A. Anthony Kennedy
B. Sandra Day O'Connor
C. William Rehnquist
D. Antonin Scalia

11.24 The Corsican National Liberation Front wants the island
of Corsica to secede from what country? [58]
A. France
B. Greece
C. Italy
D. Spain

11.25 Who was the first president to appoint a Hispanic to the
cabinet? [29]
A. George Bush
B. Jimmy Carter
C. Ronald Reagan
D. Theodore Roosevelt

11.26 Clint Eastwood was once elected mayor of what
California town? [85]
A. Beverly Hills
B. Carmel
C. Monterey
D. San Jose

11.27 A "jezebel" is a shameless hussy. Where did the original
Jezebel first appear? [52]
A. the Bible
B. a Charles Dickens story
C. a Shakespearean play
D. a silent film

11.28 Which science-fiction TV series featured villains called
"Nestenes"? [7]
A. *Battlestar Galactica*
B. *Doctor Who*
C. *Lost in Space*
D. *Star Trek: The Next Generation*

11.29 According to Homer's epic poem *The Iliad*, who or what
was inside the Trojan Horse? [65]
A. Greek soldiers
B. Trojan soldiers
C. horses
D. nothing

11.30 Which family member was played by Michael Learned
on the long-running TV drama *The Waltons*? [20]
A. Esther
B. John-Boy
C. Olivia
D. Zeb

11.31 Under the German Reinheitsgebot, or "purity command,"
the only ingredients from which beer may be made are
water and all but which of the following? [34]
A. hops
B. malt
C. rice
D. yeast

11.32 The Amazon rain forest has existed since the end of the
Pleistocene epoch, or for about how many years? [74]
A. 10,000
B. 100,000
C. 1,000,000
D. 10,000,000

11.33 What golfer won the Masters twice and the British Open twice during the period 1987–1990? [45]
  A. Nick Faldo
  B. Scott Hoch
  C. Greg Norman
  D. Curtis Strange

11.34 Who created the creatures known as "Fraggles"? [67]
  A. Lewis Carroll
  B. the Brothers Grimm
  C. Jim Henson
  D. Dr. Seuss

11.35 In the original 1933 movie *King Kong*, what was the name of the island on which the great ape was discovered? [5]
  A. Ape Island
  B. Borneo
  C. Monster Island
  D. Skull Island

11.36 Which pair of genetically similar characters perform a piano duet in the movie *Who Framed Roger Rabbit?* [23]
  A. Bambi and Bullwinkle
  B. Donald Duck and Daffy Duck
  C. Garfield and Sylvester
  D. Speedy Gonzales and Minnie Mouse

11.37 What team won the first two Superbowls, in 1967 and 1968? [48]
  A. Cleveland Browns
  B. Dallas Cowboys
  C. Green Bay Packers
  D. Pittsburgh Steelers

11.38 Who wrote the poem beginning "When I was one-and-twenty/I heard a wise man say"? [94]
  A. Robert Browning
  B. Lewis Carroll
  C. A.E. Housman
  D. Rudyard Kipling

11.39 The pay-per-view cable TV fee—$34.95—to watch an event that took place on June 27, 1988, was the highest fee ever paid at that time. What was the event? [38]
A. the baseball All-Star Game
B. the Indianapolis 500 auto race
C. the Kentucky Derby horse race
D. the Tyson-Spinks heavyweight fight

11.40 Which of these four poets was male? [81]
A. Emily Dickinson
B. Joyce Kilmer
C. Amy Lowell
D. Alice Duer Miller

11.41 Which of these celebrities was *not* born during the 1960s? [16]
A. Tom Cruise
B. Daryl Hannah
C. Madonna
D. Randy Travis

11.42 Russian novelist Leo Tolstoy was a member of nobility. What title often preceded his name? [8]
A. Baron
B. Count
C. Duke
D. Marquis

11.43 The term "White House" did not become official until Theodore Roosevelt was in office, but other presidents had already lived there for over a century. What president was the first to live there? [95]
A. George Washington
B. John Adams
C. Thomas Jefferson
D. James Madison

11.44 The people of Palau, the world's last United Nations
Trust Territory, voted for self-government in 1987,
although Palau's former owner will retain control of its
defenses. What is this former owner? [51]
   A. Japan
   B. Soviet Union
   C. United Kingdom
   D. United States

11.45 Which of the following books was *not* written by Charles
Dickens? [78]
   A. *Barchester Towers*
   B. *Dombey and Son*
   C. *Great Expectations*
   D. *Hard Times*

11.46 Jimmy Page was the guitarist of what group, which
disbanded after the death of its drummer John Bonham in
1980? [35]
   A. Blood, Sweat and Tears
   B. Led Zeppelin
   C. The Moody Blues
   D. The Who

11.47 What is the meaning of the title of the 1920s hit song
"Volare"? [19]
   A. to dance
   B. to fly
   C. to kiss
   D. to sing

11.48 When she married heavyweight champion Mike Tyson,
Robin Givens was a regular on what TV series? [80]
   A. *A Different World*
   B. *Head of the Class*
   C. *The Young and the Restless*
   D. *21 Jump Street*

11.49 The population of the world has increased steadily for a
long time. Approximately when did it reach 100 million
persons? [59]
   A. 15,000 B.C.
   B. 3000 B.C.
   C. 300 A.D.
   D. 1500 A.D.

11.50 Where, in 1846, was the first documented baseball game
played that used the modern rules and field layout
developed by Alexander Cartwright? [41]
   A. Boston, Massachusetts
   B. Cooperstown, New York
   C. Hoboken, New Jersey
   D. London, England

11.51 What musical provided Barbara Cook with two of her
most popular songs, "Dear Friend" and "Vanilla Ice
Cream"? [72]
   A. *Candide*
   B. *Carousel*
   C. *The Music Man*
   D. *She Loves Me*

11.52 "Little-box-you-push-him-he-cry-out-little-box-you-pull-
him-he-cry-out" is pidgin English for what musical
instrument? [93]
   A. accordion
   B. bagpipes
   C. trombone
   D. tuba

11.53 The pit of what fruit is the source of the controversial
cancer-treating drug known as Laetrile? [55]
   A. apricot
   B. cherry
   C. peach
   D. watermelon

11.54 In a description of wine, which of these is *not* a favorable
adjective? [26]
- **A.** fat
- **B.** flinty
- **C.** leggy
- **D.** vigorous

11.55 What are *The Card Party, Filling Station, The Footballer*,
and *Wedding Breakfast at the Eiffel Tower* all titles of?
[62]
- **A.** ballets
- **B.** French paintings
- **C.** pop record albums
- **D.** short stories by O'Henry

11.56 Which of these "tough-guy" actors was born with the
middle name DeForest? [90]
- **A.** Humphrey Bogart
- **B.** James Cagney
- **C.** Clint Eastwood
- **D.** Burt Lancaster

11.57 According to *Harper's Index Book*, what is the most
popular name for a dog in the U.S.? [43]
- **A.** Fluffy
- **B.** Max
- **C.** Rover
- **D.** Spot

11.58 According to the Bible, what destroyed the cities of
Sodom and Gomorrah? [99]
- **A.** an earthquake
- **B.** fire and brimstone
- **C.** a flood
- **D.** a volcano

11.59 Where would you see a "flying buttress"? [56]
- **A.** at an airport
- **B.** at a football game
- **C.** on a building
- **D.** underwater

11.60 What car advertises itself as "the ultimate driving machine"? [6]
 A. BMW
 B. Mercedes
 C. Volkswagen
 D. Volvo

11.61 What is the title of Judy Oppenheimer's 1988 biography of Shirley Jackson, the 20th-century writer who is best remembered for her 1948 short story "The Lottery"? [32]
 A. *Fire and Ice*
 B. *Hill House Blues*
 C. *Private Demons*
 D. *Shirley, Shirley*

11.62 What kind of nut is used to make marzipan? [49]
 A. almond
 B. cashew
 C. pecan
 D. walnut

11.63 What is the last letter of the Greek alphabet? [4]
 A. alpha
 B. omega
 C. upsilon
 D. zeta

11.64 What U.S. corporation has the largest number of stockholders? [71]
 A. AT&T
 B. General Motors
 C. IBM
 D. Xerox

11.65 Which of these is generally *not* an ingredient in the sandwich known as a "Reuben"? [89]
 A. boiled ham
 B. corned beef
 C. sauerkraut
 D. Swiss cheese

11.66 What character in TV advertisements has been portrayed by David Leisure? [39]
   A. Joe Isuzu
   B. the Man from G.L.A.D.
   C. the Maytag Repairman
   D. Mr. Whipple

11.67 Which of these animals is *not* one of the 12 that appears as a "Year of the ..." on the Chinese calendar? [97]
   A. Duck
   B. Monkey
   C. Pig
   D. Snake

11.68 What Biblical character owned a coat of many colors? [86]
   A. Jacob
   B. Jesus
   C. Jonah
   D. Joseph

11.69 Whose real name is Charles Carter? [12]
   A. actor Charlton Heston
   B. actor Chuck Norris
   C. bodybuilder Charles Atlas
   D. former president Jimmy Carter

11.70 All Saints' Day, previously known as All Hallows' Day, is a holiday in parts of Europe. What is its date? [79]
   A. February 2
   B. May 2
   C. July 14
   D. November 1

11.71 What are you saying when you write a "bread-and-butter" note? [54]
   A. I'm sorry.
   B. Thank you.
   C. We've moved.
   D. You're invited for dinner.

11.72 Which was *not* one of Gregor Mendel's laws of heredity? [96]
    A. dominance
    B. independent assortment
    C. integration
    D. segregation

11.73 The original Bellini, invented in Venice, Italy, in 1931, was a mixture of sparkling Italian white wine and what fruit juice? [73]
    A. apple
    B. orange
    C. peach
    D. pomegranate

11.74 What pair of countries trade with each other the most, as measured by the value of the goods they sell to one another? [30]
    A. the Soviet Union and China
    B. the Soviet Union and East Germany
    C. the United States and Canada
    D. the United States and Japan

11.75 Which of the following is *not* one of the children of Prince Rainier of Monaco? [76]
    A. Prince Albert
    B. Princess Anne
    C. Princess Caroline
    D. Princess Stephanie

11.76 About how many pet birds are there in the U.S.? [14]
    A. 45,000
    B. 450,000
    C. 4,500,000
    D. 45,000,000

11.77 In driving from Canada to Mexico, what is the smallest number of states you can possibly pass through? [1]
    A. 3
    B. 4
    C. 5
    D. 6

11.78 Who wrote the controversial 1988 book *Being a Woman,*
Fulfilling Your Femininity and Finding Love? [53]
   A. Dr. Joyce Brothers
   B. Dr. Toni Grant
   C. Ann Landers
   D. Dr. Ruth Westheimer

11.79 Which of the following has *not* been approved for use in
the United States as an artificial sweetener? [25]
   A. acesulfame K
   B. acetaminophen
   C. aspartame
   D. saccharine

11.80 Which of these women did *not* win the Miss America
crown? [100]
   A. Lee Meriwether
   B. Mary Ann Mobley
   C. Jaclyn Smith
   D. Vanessa Williams

11.81 How many points did the Dow Jones Industrial Average
drop on October 19, 1987, when it set a record for the
most points lost in a single day? [47]
   A. 208
   B. 508
   C. 808
   D. 1,108

11.82 On TV's *The Love Boat*, what was Adam Bricker's job on
the ship? [11]
   A. bartender
   B. captain
   C. doctor
   D. social director

11.83 What IRS form do employees fill out so that their
employers can determine the correct amount of federal
income tax to withhold from their pay? [83]
   A. W-2
   B. W-4
   C. 1040
   D. 1099

11.84 Which TV cop duo were secretly married to one another?
[42]
  A. Cagney and Lacey
  B. Holmes and YoYo
  C. Magruder and Loud
  D. Starsky and Hutch

11.85 The world's longest railroad tunnel, over 33 miles long, is
the Seikan, in what country? [91]
  A. Japan
  B. Soviet Union
  C. Switzerland
  D. United States

11.86 Which of the following is *not* owned by Pepsico? [27]
  A. Betty Crocker products
  B. Doritos chips
  C. Frito-Lay snacks
  D. Pizza Hut

11.87 By the end of 1900, how many cars were on the road in
the United States? [61]
  A. 138
  B. 1,380
  C. 13,800
  D. 138,000

11.88 What 1987 movie was based on Gustav Hasford's novel
The Short Timers? [98]
  A. *Angel Heart*
  B. *Broadcast News*
  C. *Fatal Attraction*
  D. *Full Metal Jacket*

11.89 A mosque that will be the largest in Europe is under
construction in what city? [50]
  A. London
  B. Madrid
  C. Paris
  D. Rome

11.90 According to polls, which of these presidents had the
highest overall approval rating after one year in office?
[88]
A. George Bush
B. Jimmy Carter
C. Richard Nixon
D. Ronald Reagan

11.91 When the luxury liner *S.S. Titanic* sank in 1912, how
many of the 2,224 persons aboard survived? [9]
A. none
B. about a third
C. about two-thirds
D. all but one

11.92 Which of the following pitchers had the most World
Scrics victories? [28]
A. Don Drysdale
B. Whitey Ford
C. Sandy Koufax
D. Don Larsen

11.93 In 1985, a song titled "Party All the Time" reached the
number two position on *Billboard's* pop charts. Which
alumnus of *Saturday Night Live* recorded this song? [77]
A. Garrett Morris
B. Eddie Murphy
C. Bill Murray
D. Joe Piscopo

11.94 Which of the following Broadway musicals did *not*
originally star Ethel Merman? [37]
A. *Annie Get Your Gun*
B. *Anything Goes*
C. *Call Me Madam*
D. *Pal Joey*

11.95 Who wrote the Declaration of Independence? [2]
A. Benjamin Franklin
B. Thomas Jefferson
C. James Madison
D. George Washington

11.96 Which of the following countries does *not* border France? [92]
A. Belgium
B. Luxembourg
C. The Netherlands
D. Switzerland

11.97 How much time in prison did Oliver North have to serve after his 1989 trial on Iran-Contra charges? [15]
A. none
B. 30 days
C. 6 months
D. 10 years

11.98 Who wrote the classic science fiction novel *The Invisible Man*? [84]
A. Robert Louis Stevenson
B. Jules Verne
C. H.G. Wells
D. Oscar Wilde

11.99 According to the *Nielsen Television Report*, about how many hours per day is the average TV set on? [33]
A. 1
B. 4
C. 7
D. 12

11.100 In the Australian song "Waltzing Matilda," who or what is Matilda? [68]
A. a boat
B. a girl
C. a kangaroo
D. a knapsack

11.101 What is the last line spoken in the *Star Wars* film trilogy? [22]
A. "Good-bye."
B. "Good luck."
C. "He's my brother."
D. "May the force be with you."

Answers

Within each chapter, answers have been scrambled to prevent players from accidentally seeing the answer to the next question. The number that appears in brackets after each question is the number of the answer as it appears within its chapter section here.

Answers to Chapter 2: Question Sets

1. **F** (Hawaii)
2. **T** (Insurance for the paintings, worth hundreds of millions of dollars, would have cost around $3 million a year—more than the museum's operating budget.)
3. **A**
4. **C** (China is second, followed by Poland.)
5. **C**
6. **D** (He hit a record 56 home runs in 1930.)
7. **F** (The movie was released a few days before the Three Mile Island accident.)
8. **T**
9. **F** (It's the British newspaper establishment.)
10. **B**
11. **C**
12. **B**
13. **T**
14. **B**
15. **B**
16. **T**
17. **T** (over a quarter trillion made)
18. **A**
19. **B**
20. **B**
21. **F** (Long before *Dallas* was *Peyton Place*, 1964-69.)
22. **F** (It's 26 miles, 385 yards.)

23. **D**
24. **D**
25. **D**
26. **T**   (Bela Karolyi, who defected from Romania in between the two championships)
27. **C**
28. **C**
29. **F**   (The record is four, held by several players. John tied the record for pitchers, though. All three of his errors, by the way, came on the same play.)
30. **F**   (Verdi lived to be 88.)
31. **B**   (Cy Young had 511 career victories and Walter Johnson had 416.)
32. **C**   (from 17% to 68%)
33. **C**   (from August 1977 to August 1989)
34. **T**
35. **B**
36. **T**   (by about 985 feet to 555 feet)
37. **C**   (His real name was Merwyn Bogue.)
38. **T**   (That year, Leonardo was 48 years old, and Michelangelo was 25.)
39. **T**   (while Franklin Pierce was president, 1853-57)
40. **D**
41. **C**
42. **A**
43. **T**   (Al Joyner is both Griffith Joyner's husband and Jackie Joyner-Kersee's brother.)
44. **C**
45. **F**   (Brian Lawton was, by Minnesota in 1983.)
46. **B**
47. **B**
48. **A**
49. **F**   (In 1985, for example, there was an all-Missouri World Series between the Kansas City Royals and the St. Louis Cardinals. Previously, there were all-Chicago and all-St. Louis World Series.)
50. **D**
51. **F**   (It's the same.)
52. **F**   (It's from George Orwell's *Animal House*.)
53. **F**   (It took place two years before.)
54. **C**   (As of 1990, with about 29% of all foreign investment in the U.S.; Japan is second, with around 16 percent.)
55. **B**

56. **A**
57. **T**
58. **B**
59. **C**
60. **A**
61. **T**
62. **F** (It doesn't stand for anything in particular.)
63. **F** (It was written by Samuel Pepys.)
64. **B**
65. **C**
66. **C**
67. **B** (He once led the league in homers while batting only .204.)
68. **B**
69. **T**
70. **A** (93.75%, compared with Palmer's 92.5%)
71. **B**
72. **F** (Barbra Streisand, for example, won for her screen debut in *Funny Girl*.)
73. **F**
74. **A**
75. **A**
76. **F** (Honda Accord, in 1989, was the first foreign car to achieve this honor.)
77. **C** (though he lived in the other two states later)
78. **B**
79. **D**
80. **C** (Diamond is for 30th or 60th, emerald for 55th.)
81. **A** (about 38%)
82. **D**
83. **A**
84. **C**
85. **T** (But her album *Tapestry*, which included that hit, was a number one selling album for a long time.)
86. **F** (Mohammed is more common, and is probably the most common.)
87. **T** (Dwight D. Eisenhower named it for his grandson.)
88. **F** (15 pieces)
89. **F** (It means "cheeseburger.")
90. **C**
91. **C**
92. **C** (It can run the distance at about 60 m.p.h., more than 10 m.p.h. faster than a racehorse. Lions can go about 50 m.p.h.,

but only for short distances, and giraffes are quite a bit
slower.)
93. **C**   (Overall, it went from 4 cents to 25 cents.)
94. **F**   (The movie is set "a long time ago.")
95. **T**
96. **F**   (They don't drink at all, and get all their moisture from the
eucalyptus leaves they eat.)
97. **B**
98. **D**   (It increased from $30,000 to nearly $600,000.)
99. **C**
100. **T**   (It was completed in 1903.)
101. **B**   (Budweiser alone accounted for 27% of the market.)
102. **D**
103. **C**
104. **T**
105. **T**   (Since ice is less dense than water, it floats on it.)
106. **F**   (Cymbeline is, for example.)
107. **C**
108. **C**
109. **C**   (on the 12th hole at Augusta, tying the record of Tsuneyuki
Nakajima)
110. **C**
111. **B**
112. **C**   (Liza Minnelli starred in the movie version.)
113. **F**   (Doctors do.)
114. **T**
115. **B**
116. **A**
117. **D**
118. **A**
119. **D**   (Wales and Campbell are the conference names; the other
division is Norris.)
120. **C**
121. **F**   (He was never in the armed forces.)
122. **T**   (Offspring of guppies, surf-perches, and certain other fish
hatch inside the mother.)
123. **A**   (It had 22 bottling plants there at the time.)
124. **A**   (Malawi's population without the refugees was only 7.5
million.)
125. **B**   (A rare exception was 1983, when it was played at the Rose
Bowl in Pasadena, California.)
126. **T**

127. **F**   (Bulls cannot distinguish one color from another. A matador's red cape attracts them because of its movement.)

128. **A**

129. **B**   (In 1876 and 1888, the popular vote winners lost in the electoral college; in 1824, no one got a majority of electors—though Jackson led—and the House of Representatives elected Adams.)

130. **B**

131. **B**

132. **F**   (She was burned at the stake.)

133. **T**

134. **F**   (Augustus, or Octavian, Caesar became the first in 27 B.C., 17 years after Julius's death.)

135. **C**

136. **A**

137. **B**

138. **D**

139. **A**

140. **A**

141. **B**

142. **B**

143. **A**

144. **B**   ($120,000 in 1991, with increases scheduled; baseball's is $100,000, while football was only $50,000 as of 1990.)

145. **C**

146. **D**

147. **C**

148. **T**

149. **T**   (The World Cup started in 1930, the Indianapolis 500 in 1909, and the Tour de France in 1903.)

150. **B**   (Hawaii is on Aleutian-Hawaii Time, which is two hours earlier than Pacific Time.)

151. **C**

152. **A**   (The postal abbreviation for Minnesota is MN; for Mississippi, MS; and for Missouri, MO.)

153. **B**

154. **B**

155. **C**   (1981-1989 seasons; Lambert did make it nine times in a row, though not in his first nine years.)

156. **D**

157. **C**

158. **A**

159. **F** (It was from a dying statement of James Lawrence, captain of the *U.S.S. Chesapeake* in the War of 1812.)

160. **A**

161. **B**

162. **C**

163. **F** (It did not free slaves in Union states, such as Kentucky and Maryland.)

164. **T**

165. **D**

166. **C**

167. **T** (Wombats are animals of Australia, and all land creatures were created on the sixth day.)

168. **D**

169. **C**

170. **B** (It's from *Milk and Honey*.)

171. **C**

172. **F** (The Eastern Time Zone does.)

173. **B**

174. **T**

175. **C**

176. **F** (They may not carry firearms for any reason.)

177. **B**

178. **F** (They're by Johann Sebastian Bach.)

179. **A**

180. **T**

181. **D**

182. **F** (He strikes out.)

183. **C**

184. **D**

185. **C**

186. **B** (Henderson, as an Oakland Athletic in 1982, stole 130 bases.)

187. **A** (She was fashion editor of *Harper's Bazaar*, then editor-in-chief of *Vogue*.)

188. **B**

189. **B**

190. **B**

191. **C**

192. **D**

193. **B**

194. **F** (The South Pole was reached in 1911, but by a Norwegian team led by Roald Amundsen.)

195. **C**

196. **F**

197. **C**
198. **F** (They're from a poem commonly called "Invictus" by William Ernest Henley.)
199. **B**
200. **D** (Robie's Clock, Cube, and Magic are registered trademarks.)
201. **T**
202. **D**
203. **T** (Some pirated copies are available, however.)
204. **D**
205. **A**
206. **C** James Madison (He led troops during the War of 1812, while trying to defend Washington, D.C. against the invading British.)
207. **C**
208. **F** (It never stops growing.)
209. **T**
210. **A**
211. **B**
212. **C**
213. **T**
214. **F** (Some opossums, which are marsupials, live in the wild in North America.)
215. **C** (The same is true of the related "platinum group" metals: palladium, rhodium, ruthenium, iridium, and osmium.)
216. **C**
217. **C** (nearly $138 million, an average salary of $485,506 per player per year)
218. **A**
219. **C**
220. **A**
221. **A**
222. **F** (It is third, after Spain and Italy.)
223. **F** (A furlong is an eighth of a mile.)
224. **F** (There has never been a movie called *Navarone Sunday*.)
225. **C** (in 1937 and 1938, for *Captains Courageous* and *Boys Town*)
226. **T** (They weigh around 150 tons, about double the estimated weight of the largest dinosaur, the brachiosaurus.)
227. **C**
228. **T**
229. **B**
230. **C**
231. **T**
232. **B**

233. **B**   (1975 and 1976)
234. **A**
235. **C**
236. **B**   ($399 million at the beginning of 1990; second, *Star Wars*, $322 million)
237. **A**
238. **F**   (They declined each year.)
239. **B**
240. **D**   (*Poltergeist III*, not *Poltergeist II*, was a 1988 film.)
241. **B**
242. **D**
243. **C**
244. **B**
245. **B**
246. **A**   (A 42% percent increase; Arizona and Nevada were second and third, each over 34%. Florida increased by almost 32%.)
247. **A**
248. **A**
249. **C**
250. **B**

Answers to Chapter 3: Entertainment, Literature, and Art

1. **B**
2. **F**   (Jane Austen was just Jane Austen.)
3. **F**   ("Sweet Valley Twins" novels are for preteens.)
4. **A**   (Klaatu is the alien; Robby is the robot in another acclaimed '50s film, *Forbidden Planet*.)
5. **C**
6. **F**   (She did accomplish this, in 1967 and 1968 for *Guess Who's Coming to Dinner?* and *The Lion in Winter*; but Luise Rainer also did it in 1936 and 1937 for *The Great Ziegfeld* and *The Good Earth*.)
7. **A**
8. **A**   (The same year, Bugs Bunny turned 50 and Fred Flintstone turned 30.)
9. **F**   (Novelettes, defined as 7,500-17,500 words, are shorter than novellas, defined as 17,500-40,000 words.)
10. **C**   (Bugs's line "Gee, ain't I a stinker?" came from Costello.)
11. **D**

12. **F**   (At the end of the film, Bambi becomes a father.)
13. **B**
14. **D**
15. **C**
16. **F**   (It was written by John Gardner.)
17. **A**
18. **A**
19. **A**
20. **B**
21. **A**   (All were born in, and died in, that century.)
22. **T**
23. **C**   (At a time when the American comic strips were hard to come by in much of Europe.)
24. **T**
25. **B**
26. **C**
27. **A**   (in *A Connecticut Yankee in King Arthur's Court*)
28. **T**
29. **B**   (Edmond Rostand's 1897 play *Cyrano de Bergerac* was loosely based on his life.)
30. **B**
31. **C**
32. **F**
33. **A**
34. **F**   (It's based on several comedies of Plautus.)
35. **T**
36. **B**   ($125 million. Steven Spielberg was second, with $105 million; Cosby third with $95 million. Winfrey earned $55 million, and Madonna earned $43 million.)
37. **F**   (He wrote it in New York City.)
38. **C**
39. **F**   (It won for best art direction.)
40. **B**
41. **T**
42. **T**   (David Morrell)
43. **C**
44. **C**   (played by Robert DeNiro and Charles Grodin)
45. **T**   (The film was *The Killers*, a 1964 release.)
46. **A**
47. **A**   (*The Donna Reed Show* was set in Hilldale.)
48. **C**   (Voltaire, or Francois Marie Arouet, studied law but dropped it. He never studied medicine.)
49. **B**

50. **B**
51. **T**   (in 1988)
52. **B**
53. **C**   (Fortunately, she recovered.)
54. **D**   (John Forsythe was Charlie.)
55. **T**   ("Three Stars Will Shine Tonight")
56. **A**
57. **B**
58. **C**
59. **C**
60. **C**
61. **T**
62. **C**   (It was bought by Ryoei Saito, a Japanese businessman.)
63. **B**
64. **B**
65. **T**
66. **F**   (Kathleen Turner does the speaking voice, but Amy Irving does her singing.)
67. **A**
68. **B**   (His father was Australian, and they moved back there when he was 12.)
69. **A**
70. **F**   (his daughter.)
71. **T**
72. **B**
73. **B**   (for *The Accused*)
74. **C**
75. **F**   (It means "becoming quieter.")

Answers to Chapter 4: Geography and Sightseeing

1. **B**
2. **D**
3. **A**   (in Wyoming, established 1906)
4. **C**
5. **B**
6. **T**   (Eastern)
7. **F**   (New England is larger, by about 67,000 square miles to 50,000 square miles.)
8. **T**
9. **B**

10. **B**   (The capital of Maryland is Annapolis.)
11. **F**   (There are 10 Canadian provinces and 15 Soviet Republics.)
12. **C**
13. **B**   (Agana is the capital of Guam, and Pago Pago is the capital of American Samoa.)
14. **B**   (Its highest point is only 345 feet above sea level.)
15. **T**
16. **A**
17. **T**
18. **A**   (It's only about 14 ft wide and 6 feet long.)
19. **B**
20. **B**   (31,700 square miles)
21. **D**   (11,009 miles apart)
22. **C**
23. **A**   (in North Carolina and Tennessee, with nearly 9 million visitors a year)
24. **A**
25. **T**   (583 miles, compared with 714)
26. **C**
27. **F**
28. **F**   (The average depth of the Pacific is 12,925 feet; in the Atlantic, it's 11,730 feet.)
29. **C**
30. **F**   (The largest is Wrangell-St. Elias in Alaska, which is more than five times larger than Yellowstone's 2.2 million acres.)
31. **T**
32. **C**
33. **C**
34. **T**
35. **A**
36. **T**
37. **C**   (Mount Aconcagua, in Argentina , 22,834 feet high)
38. **C**
39. **C**
40. **C**
41. **B**
42. **C**   (Lake Ontario borders only New York, and Lake Huron only Michigan.)
43. **C**
44. **C**   (Zambesia is the name of a province in Mozambique.)
45. **F**   (Australia is the smallest.)
46. **B**
47. **F**   (The capital is the largest city in only 14 of 50 states.)

48. **C**
49. **B**
50. **A**   (There is a Northern Territory, but it is a territory, not a state.)
51. **B**
52. **D**   (4,876 miles apart)
53. **B**
54. **F**   (Canada is still larger.)
55. **T**
56. **T**
57. **A**
58. **A**
59. **D**   (The U.S. 18- to 24-year-olds did worse than persons of the same age in any of the other eight countries tested—Canada, France, Italy, Japan, Mexico, Sweden, United Kingdom, and West Germany. Sweden did the best.)
60. **F**   (Though both are in California.)
61. **B**
62. **F**   (New Delhi is the capital, but Calcutta is the largest city.)
63. **F**
64. **A**
65. **C**
66. **T**   (The distance to Tokyo is 3,859 miles; to New York, it's 4,969 miles.)
67. **F**   (Illinois and Indiana, for example, border each other.)
68. **C**
69. **C**
70. **A**
71. **B**
72. **A**   (Baffin, Victoria, and Ellesmere. Of the other islands among the 10 largest, Indonesia owns all of one, Sumatra, but only parts of two, New Guinea and Borneo.)
73. **F**   (It is 605 feet tall, but two Seattle skyscrapers are taller.)
74. **F**   (Kansas's highest point is higher, by 4,039 feet to 3,560 feet.)
75. **A**

Answers to Chapter 5: History and Demographics

1. **B**
2. **T**   (From 46 to 44 B.C.; she was queen from 51 to 30 B.C.)
3. **A**
4. **T**   (in 1902)

5. **B**

6. **C**

7. **T**

8. **B** (The explosion leveled 230 square miles.)

9. **T**

10. **C** (more than a 10% increase)

11. **C**

12. **A**

13. **D**

14. **T** (He turned it down.)

15. **C** (25.7 years of age; Alaska was second youngest.)

16. **B**

17. **D** (Stanley found Livingstone in 1871.)

18. **T** (She lived to be 97.)

19. **A**

20. **F** (It was the other way around.)

21. **A**

22. **T** (his brother Robert, as attorney-general)

23. **C**

24. **D**

25. **A**

26. **B** (in Nicaragua)

27. **D** (A total of eight. Next is Ohio, with seven.)

28. **B**

29. **A** (15,556, more than twice the number in any year since 1970)

30. **F** (It lasted 116 years.)

31. **T** (about 52%)

32. **D**

33. **F** (The U.S. did, but Switzerland has never joined.)

34. **C**

35. **F** (John Turner was prime minister in between.)

36. **A**

37. **B** (The French-Canadians, who were Acadians, are known as Cajuns.)

38. **D**

39. **D**

40. **B** (almost exactly: 50.0%)

41. **T** (The number of people in this age group declined more than 8 percent.)

42. **A**

43. **B**

44. **D**

45. **C** (50.8 percent. When the figure was first calculated in 1976, it was just 31 percent.)
46. **T** (From 2.8 to 2.6. The number of households went up 17 percent, while the population only went up 10 percent.)
47. **A**
48. **T**
49. **C**
50. **T** (Over 270,000 barrels spilled immediately; more leaked later.)
51. **T**
52. **C** (It lasted from 1821 to 1918.)
53. **C** (King of ancient Israel in the 10th century B.C.; Confucius lived in the 6th and 5th centuries B.C., and Plato a century later.)
54. **F** (He entered New York Harbor.)
55. **A** (He stepped down in 1986.)
56. **T** (Dukakis regained the governorship in the 1982 election.)
57. **C** (which is the former name of Volgograd)
58. **A** (36.4 years of age; New Jersey was second oldest.)
59. **C** (in 1791)
60. **C**
61. **F** (It guaranteed certain civil liberties for the Protestant Huguenots.)
62. **T** (The number was 13 originally, but had increased to 15 after the admission of two more states.)
63. **F**
64. **C**
65. **B** (16.9%, compared to 6% of governors and 5.2% of Congress)
66. **A**
67. **C**
68. **T**
69. **T** (She died in January, 1901, at age 81, after ruling 59 years.)
70. **A** (Known then as South-West Africa, it was seized from Germany by South Africa during World War I.)
71. **T** (It's the real name of Gerald Ford.)
72. **D**
73. **B**
74. **C** (The dynasty ran from 1368-1644.)
75. **B**

Answers to Chapter 6: Science and Nature

1. **F**　(A female cosmonaut named Savitskaya walked in space in 1984.)
2. **A**　(Nor will one ever land there, since the planet is entirely gaseous.)
3. **D**　(Certain other house plants were found to help clean the air, too.)
4. **A**
5. **C**
6. **A**　(It was developed between 1923 and 1927, though commercial broadcasts did not start until later.)
7. **F**　(It leaves many alive, some of which aid in the digestion of the milk.)
8. **B**
9. **A**　(based on the Mohs hardness scale)
10. **C**
11. **C**　(Mercury, Venus, Mars, Pluto)
12. **T**
13. **A**
14. **T**
15. **F**　(It's laughing gas.)
16. **C**
17. **B**　(1860; then aspirin in 1889, penicillin in 1929)
18. **T**　(A minority of centipedes, though, do have as many as 200 legs.)
19. **B**
20. **B**　(The symbols for the others are Ca for calcium, Cl for chlorine, and Cu for copper.)
21. **D**
22. **A**
23. **A**
24. **B**
25. **B**　(In elliptical geometry—on the surface of a sphere, for example—the sum is always more, while in hyperbolic geometry it is always less.)
26. **T**
27. **F**
28. **A**　(Of the three, polar bears weigh the most.)
29. **T**　(This was discovered in 1940, but the reasons are still not fully understood.)
30. **C**

31. **B**

32. **D**   (Complex numbers include real numbers, imaginary numbers, and numbers that are sums of the two.)

33. **T**

34. **C**   (Forty-nine were discovered then. Most of the others—there are now over 100—were discovered in the 18th and 20th centuries, though some have been known since ancient times.)

35. **A**

36. **C**

37. **T**   (Apparently after being knocked free of the moon's gravity by meteorite impacts there. A number of these have been found in Antarctica.)

38. **C**   (The other kinds mentioned are also quarks, but exist only in cosmic rays or particle accelerators.)

39. **A**

40. **B**   (Charge is usually measured in coulombs, field strength in volts per meter, and potential in volts.)

41. **C**

42. **T**   (typically, between 50 percent and 100 percent of its weight)

43. **A**   (about 60-65 calories, compared with 80 for the sugar and 100 for the milk)

44. **F**   (A sponge is an animal.)

45. **C**   (The ship would gain mass, even though it diminished in size.)

46. **D**

47. **T**

48. **A**

49. **T**   (about 660 per hour vs. 600 per hour)

50. **C**

51. **F**   (Both travel at the speed of light.)

52. **C**   (There are 8 bits in a byte, and 1,024 bytes in a kilobyte.)

53. **C**

54. **D**

55. **F**   (Elephants' average life spans are 35 to 40 years, depending upon the breed of elephant.)

56. **C**   (about 7 years; gray squirrel 10, moose 12, grizzly bear 25)

57. **F**   (It appears as a half moon.)

58. **T**   (due to a stomach enzyme that men have more of, which breaks down more of the alcohol before it reaches the bloodstream)

59. **A**

60. **F**   (They typically spend their entire lives within 125 yards of their birthplace.)
61. **C**
62. **T**
63. **F**   (The joint cracked is not one where wear-and-tear-type arthritis tends to develop.)
64. **B**   (in 1885; smallpox, by Jenner in 1796; polio, by Salk in 1953)
65. **F**   (K is the symbol for potassium; Kr is krypton's symbol.)
66. **C**   (Oxygen is second with 21 percent.)
67. **C**
68. **B**
69. **A**   (In a lunar eclipse, the earth's shadow covers the moon's surface.)
70. **C**
71. **B**   (Yellow is one of the primary colors of pigments, along with cyan and magenta.)
72. **F**   (It freezes at about −259 degrees Celsius.)
73. **B**
74. **F**   (It travels about five times faster underwater.)
75. **D**   (It's the formula for Epsom salts.)

Answers to Chapter 7: Sports and Games

1. **F**   (He sired over 400 foals.)
2. **A**   (next oldest is Comiskey Park, built 1910)
3. **D**
4. **F**   (Roberto Clemente did in 1967, and Dave Parker in 1977.)
5. **B**
6. **A**   (in 1987)
7. **T**   (a 7–6 victory over Oregon in 1920)
8. **A**
9. **C**   (47,003; Jabbar scored 44,149 points, while Shoemaker took 40,350 rides—winning 8,833, by the way)
10. **B**   (by hitting the triple 20)
11. **C**   (on April 14, 1910, in Washington, D.C., at the season opener between the Washington Senators and the Philadelphia Athletics)
12. **D**   (beginning at the end of the 1988 season, ending early in the 1989 season)
13. **C**   (In other leagues, wins are worth 2, and ties 1.)
14. **T**

15. **T**

16. **C**

17. **T**   (though the opponent must not touch the net)

18. **A**   (At the time, the Olympic champion swimmer was beginning
to swim in NCAA competition for Stanford.)

19. **T**   (at age 13 years, 11 months)

20. **F**   (In 1924 he did, hitting .378 for the New York Yankees.)

21. **B**   (in 1988)

22. **C**   (Ruth began his major league career as a pitcher for the Red
Sox, and set many pitching records.)

23. **C**   (950 1/2 pounds, to be exact, breaking the old record by 276
1/2 pounds. She caught it off Hawaii's Kailua Kona coast.)

24. **C**   (over 5,000 more than his nearest rival)

25. **C**

26. **T**   (12 to 11)

27. **C**

28. **A**   (in 1945)

29. **F**   (Cy Young, who had more wins than anyone else, also lost
over 300. From 1890 to 1911, his record was 511-313.)

30. **A**

31. **A**   (52, in 1977, for the Cincinnati Reds)

32. **D**   (with Cleveland in 1960)

33. **T**   (Her 88 wins are four more than the male record, held by
Sam Snead.)

34. **B**   (1946-52 for the Pittsburgh Pirates; Ruth led the league 12
times during a 14-year stretch, but never more than six times
in a row.)

35. **C**   (in 1971, when she won $117,400 in tennis)

36. **F**   (E.g., a teammate might drop a foul pop-up for an error, but
the pitcher might get the batter out anyway. All that matters is
that none of the 27 batters reach base.)

37. **C**   (exactly)

38. **D**

39. **A**   (in 1970)

40. **F**   (It's allowed, but is under state control. Only win-place and
quinella bets are allowed.)

41. **B**   (In 1990, an appeals court held that the U.S. deserved to win
despite this irregularity.)

42. **B**   (Q, which appears in many short words such as *que* and *qui*,
is worth only 8 points. The other three letters are relatively
rare in French.)

43. **F**   (In 1989, for example, the race started in Luxembourg.)

44. **F**   (The most common nickname has been "Lefty.")

45. **B**   (three times—1983, 1987, 1989)
46. **B**   (The contract pays him $4.25 million in 1993 as part of a four-year, $15 million deal.)
47. **B**
48. **A**   (1971; Atari's Pong came next, in 1972.)
49. **T**   (He was not yet 21.)
50. **T**
51. **A**
52. **A**   (Earl Grey, in 1909)
53. **T**   (Karen and Sarah Josephson)
54. **A**   (361; then reversi—which is similar to Othello—64; Polish checkers, played on a 100-square board, 40; xiang qi, 32)
55. **A**
56. **B**   (On 98.23 percent of all ballots, the all-time record. Aaron was second best, and Johnny Bench third.)
57. **T**
58. **F**   (though he made very few of them)
59. **T**
60. **C**   ("The Wall" is a physiological phenomenon that typically hits marathon runners after 20 miles and is caused by the muscles losing an essential nutrient, glycogen. This can cause a range of symptoms, including severe cramps or increase of body temperature up to 107°.)
61. **A**   (Cincinnati's team nickname is the Bearcats.)
62. **B**
63. **F**   (There's no such rule. Most skaters do go counterclockwise, as it is more natural for most skaters to do spins in that direction.)
64. **C**   (3,308)
65. **C**   (50 times; Carey is second with 33.)
66. **A**
67. **C**
68. **T**   (Her time was 14 hours, 31 minutes, about two hours faster than the fastest time by a male swimmer.)
69. **T**   (It's 23 feet, 9 inches from the basket around the perimeter, but just 22 feet at the corners.)
70. **D**   (He won the rating 14 times between 1891 and 1920.)
71. **C**
72. **F**   (They're brothers.)
73. **B**   (ages 20 and 22, respectively, in 1965 and 1967)
74. **B**   (But if you bet $5 on the underdog, you would win back $7 instead of $8; the other dollar is the bookmaker's profit.)
75. **B**

Answers to Chapter 8: Potpourri

1. **B**
2. **A**
3. **T**   (The speed ranges from 200 r.p.m. to 500 r.p.m.)
4. **D**   ("People" is second, and "time" is third.)
5. **B**
6. **C**   (At Christie's in New York; it had been expected to sell for less than $4 million.)
7. **B**   (It had been expected to sell for only $120,000.)
8. **C**
9. **T**   (about 20 percent more)
10. **A**   (followed by bourbon and scotch)
11. **A**   (Superfine virgin is second best; there are five grades in all.)
12. **T**
13. **D**
14. **A**   (1.3; the U.S. rate was 1.9.)
15. **C**   (The Soviet Union took the region from Romania in 1940.)
16. **A**   (It was created in 1881, and P.T. Barnum's circus goes back 10 years further.)
17. **A**
18. **T**
19. **C**   (AL is Alabama, AS is American Samoa, and AA is nothing.)
20. **F**   (It's someone who hates women.)
21. **C**   ($3.0 million; Teamsters were second with $2.9 million. Trial lawyers gave $1.9 million.)
22. **T**
23. **A**
24. **D**   (The British also call it "the Wain" or "the Wagon.")
25. **T**
26. **C**
27. **T**
28. **B**
29. **C**
30. **B**
31. **C**
32. **F**   (It stands for "Organization," as in "Organization of Petroleum Exporting Countries.")
33. **F**   (Sagittarius is the Archer; Capricorn is the Goat.)
34. **T**
35. **B**
36. **C**

37. **T**   (His book *A Perfect Spy* is partly autobiographical.)
38. **B**   (He said he did it to improve security in a nearby house in which he lives.)
39. **T**   (from a diary he kept in a 1751 trip to Barbados, when he was 19)
40. **D**   (followed by peach schnapps and orange juice, margarita, and vodka and tonic)
41. **F**   (Originally, these names came from the number of lead balls, of a size that would just fit in the bore, that it took to weigh a pound. The bore diameters are now specified by international agreement.)
42. **B**   (The other juices in it are tomato, celery, lettuce, parsley, and watercress.)
43. **D**
44. **B**
45. **B**
46. **F**   (São Paolo, with more than 10 million people, is almost twice as large.)
47. **B**   (19.6%; Vermont is second, with 23.1%; Alaska, 42.4%.)
48. **D**   (in *Anna Christie*, her first "talkie")
49. **F**   (Men are eight times more likely to be colorblind than women.)
50. **C**   (in Trenton, in 1889)
51. **F**   (with spinach)
52. **C**
53. **B**
54. **T**   (The same phenomenon has been observed in all other countries where such test results have been compared, including Japan, Canada, and several European countries.)
55. **C**
56. **B**   (NoRMA is an acronym for National Retail Merchants Association, which sponsors the award along with the Newspaper Advertising Bureau.)
57. **F**   (Holly comes from holly trees.)
58. **C**   (The Cheops pyramid weighs about 5.8 million tons.)
59. **C**   (On it, for example, the standard Gregorian year 1991 falls in the year 5751 and 5752; and in the Chinese lunar calendar, most of 1991 is 4689.)
60. **A**
61. **F**   (It's still called *U.S. News & World Report*.)
62. **C**   (The letters are codes that identify the kind of plastic, for recycling purposes.)
63. **F**   (It was written by Thomas Paine.)

64. **C**
65. **A**
66. **B**
67. **F**   (Coffee came to Europe from Turkey in the l6th century; it
            had long been cultivated in Ethiopia and Arabia. It was
            introduced to Brazil in 1727.)
68. **A**   (19% of households, compared with 23% for computers and
            25% for cordless phones)
69. **F**   (Xerox does, among others.)
70. **B**
71. **D**   (late December, 1980)
72. **T**
73. **B**
74. **B**
75. **T**

Answers to Chapter 9: 1-Point Questions

1. **T**
2. **T**
3. **T**   (Henry "Light Horse Harry" Lee)
4. **T**
5. **T**   (About 70 percent are used in sodas.)
6. **T**
7. **F**   ("Xanadu," the theme from the movie of the same name,
          sung by Olivia Newton-John, made it to number eight on
          August 30, 1980.)
8. **T**   (in 1924)
9. **F**   ("Perestroika" is one of his strategies, but it means
          "restructuring," as in the economy. "Glasnost" is the term
          that means openness.)
10. **F**
11. **F**   (In 1905, when the New York Giants defeated the
           Philadelphia Athletics four games to one, all five games were
           shutouts.)
12. **T**
13. **T**
14. **T**   (On *Star Trek: The Next Generation*, one of the Enterprise's
           crewmen is a Klingon.)
15. **F**   (The first was Geraldine Ferraro.)

16. **T**   (Her mother is Sophia Loren's younger sister Maria, and her father is Mussolini's son Romano.)

17. **T**   (The other six are: the Hanging Gardens of Babylon; the Mausoleum at Halicarnassus; the Temple of Artemis at Ephesus; the Colossus of Rhodes; the Olympian Zeus statue by Phidias; and the Phares lighthouse at Alexandria; or, instead, the walls of Babylon.)

18. **T**

19. **T**

20. **T**   (It was a number one album in 1989.)

21. **T**

22. **F**   (She did appear in that movie, but had begun to appear in movies four years earlier, beginning with *Happy Land*.)

23. **F**   ("The Five Orange Pips" was one of Doyle's Holmes stories, but it was published long ago.)

24. **F**   (Bud Light)

25. **F**   (Near the end, the poem—Longfellow's "The Arrow and the Song"—says: "Long, long afterward, in an oak/I found the arrow, still unbroke.")

26. **T**

27. **F**   (There are four pecks in a bushel.)

28. **F**   (He was the first Jewish member of the Supreme Court, but was never chief justice.)

29. **T**   (If a bill that has been passed by both Houses remains with the president for 10 days—not counting Sundays—and the president neither signs it nor vetoes it, it becomes law unless Congress has adjourned.)

30. **T**

31. **F**   (It's a plant whose spices taste like a mixture of other spices.)

32. **F**   (She was acquitted.)

33. **T**

34. **T**

35. **T**   (An international foot = .3048 meters; a U.S. Survey foot = 1200/3937 meters, as defined in 1893.)

36. **T**   (Before 1500; today, they are nails that are 3 1/4 inches long.)

37. **F**   (There are about $5 billion worth of $5 bills in circulation, but only $3.7 billion worth of $1 bills.)

38. **T**   (in 1955; written by composer George Gershwin)

39. **T**

40. **T**

41. **T**

42. **F**   (The United States has never recognized the annexation, and exile groups from Latvia, as well as Lithuania and Estonia, have maintained separate diplomatic legations in the U.S. since World War II.)
43. **F**   (It means dizziness.)
44. **T**   (This was true 21 times in the first 23 years of the Super Bowl.)
45. **F**   (Europe is second, by about 680 million to 600 million, based on 1987 estimates.)
46. **F**
47. **F**   (There are 604,800 seconds in a week.)
48. **T**   (The last one, in Lansing, Michigan, closed in 1988, though five clubs in Asia remained open.)
49. **T**   (He had 24, to their 15.)
50. **F**   (The Oakland Raiders did in 1980.)
51. **F**   (It refers only to linen napkins.)
52. **F**   (A nautical mile is a little more than 6,076 feet.)
53. **F**   (It means "Okay.")
54. **T**
55. **T**
56. **F**   (They recover no faster. The only advantage of breathing oxygen appears to be psychological.)
57. **T**   (She won $134,000 as a contestant on *The $64,000 Question* and *The $64,000 Challenge*, 1955–56.)
58. **F**   (Hers did, and his didn't.)
59. **F**   (In fact, about 5% of all beverage cans are made of steel, and 95% of aluminum.)
60. **F**   (Indianapolis)
61. **F**   (It was the nickname of the frigate *U.S.S. Constitution.*)
62. **F**   (It's from *To Tell the Truth.*)
63. **T**
64. **T**   (The letters were auctioned off in 1988.)
65. **T**
66. **T**
67. **F**   (The first 90-minute western series was *The Virginian.*)
68. **T**   (The first U.S. team to join the NHL was the Boston Bruins in 1924.)
69. **T**   (He hit it in the first one ever held, in 1933.)
70. **F**   (Qatar)
71. **F**   (No star is associated with any particular state.)
72. **F**   (a degree in teaching)
73. **F**   (It originated in Europe, and was already very popular in England by the 14th century.)

74. **F**   (Robert B. Parker is.)
75. **T**
76. **T**
77. **T**   (with Horace Heidt's orchestra)
78. **F**   (E.F.O.s are "errors, freaks, and oddities," sometimes quite valuable.)
79. **F**   (The opposite is true, by $62.8 million to $38.5 million.)
80. **T**   (The movie's name is *Smiles on a Summer Night*.)
81. **F**   (She was the *youngest* of Freud's and Martha Bernay's six children.)
82. **T**
83. **T**
84. **F**   (accordion)
85. **T**
86. **T**
87. **F**   (Her father was Nehru.)
88. **T**
89. **F**   (It's Figaro.)
90. **F**   (since there is milk on Earth, and the Earth is in the Milky Way galaxy)
91. **F**   (Leonardo da Vinci painted it.)
92. **T**
93. **F**   (It's "Day.")
94. **T**
95. **T**
96. **T**
97. **F**   (One did: *Rebecca*.)
98. **F**   (Hiawatha was male.)
99. **F**   (It comes from a word meaning "quince," from which the first marmalades were made.)
100. **T**   (a cello, a viola, and two violins)

Answers to Chapter 10: 2-Point Questions

1. **B**   (Cupid was a Roman god, and Pan was god of pastures, forests, and herds.)
2. **A**
3. **B**
4. **B**   (In 1943; LaMotta was portrayed by Robert DeNiro in the film *Raging Bull*.)

5. **A**   (From the 1971-72 through 1975-76 seasons. *I Love Lucy*
            came close, with four firsts and a second in a five-year span
            in the 1950s. *The Cosby Show*, incidentally, may also have
            come in first five straight years from 1985-86 through
            1989-90, but the final year's race with *Roseanne* did not have
            a clear winner.)
6. **A**   (In 1959, the winners were Nellie Fox of the Chicago White
            Sox and Ernie Banks of the Chicago Cubs.)
7. **B**
8. **A**   (A player, though, can call time out with this signal.)
9. **B**   (Six times; he also won five PGA Championships, four U.S.
            Opens, three British Opens, and two U.S. Amateur
            Championships.)
10. **A**   ("...called for his fiddlers three")
11. **C**
12. **C**
13. **B**
14. **A**
15. **B**   (playing for the Chicago Cubs)
16. **B**
17. **C**   (They increased 96 percent; 5 to 9 year olds, just 9.8 percent,
            while 55 to 59 year olds actually decreased 8.4 percent.)
18. **B**   (in his loose translation of *The Rubaiyat of Omar Khayyám)*
19. **C**   (in 1956; Nigeria, 1960; Angola, 1975)
20. **A**
21. **C**   (He lived into his eighties.)
22. **A**
23. **A**
24. **B**
25. **A**
26. **B**
27. **A**
28. **B**
29. **B**   (probably in Mesopotamia)
30. **C**
31. **B**
32. **B**
33. **A**
34. **C**
35. **B**
36. **C**
37. **B**

38. **B**   (145 flowers per capita per year, as of 1990, compared with 40 for Japan and just 14 for the U.S.)

39. **C**

40. **A**

41. **C**

42. **B**

43. **C**

44. **B**

45. **A**

46. **B**   (in the borough of Brooklyn)

47. **B**   (Tests on humans are clinical trials.)

48. **B**

49. **C**

50. **A**

51. **A**

52. **B**

53. **A**

54. **B**

55. **C**   (Nine states start with N. The next most common first letter is M, which begins the names of eight states.)

56. **A**

57. **A**

58. **B**

59. **A**   (in 1915; Maidenform Bras, 1922; Lincoln Logs, 1924)

60. **C**

61. **A**   (You are the mortgagor.)

62. **B**

63. **A**

64. **B**

65. **C**

66. **C**

67. **C**   (1939–40, 1964–5)

68. **C**

69. **B**

70. **C**

71. **B**

72. **C**

73. **A**   (exactly)

74. **B**   (Only the year 2000. 2050 is not divisible by 4; as for 2100, years ending in 00 are only leap years if they are divisible by 400.)

75. **B**   (His 39 in 1948 were one short of Johnny Mize and Ralph Kiner that year; overall, he hit 475.)

76. **A**
77. **B**
78. **B**
79. **A**
80. **B**
81. **A**
82. **B**
83. **B**   (1985, 1986, 1987, 1988 twice, 1989)
84. **A**
85. **A**
86. **A**
87. **B**
88. **B**
89. **A**
90. **C**
91. **A**   (the Royal Perth Yacht Club, to be specific)
92. **C**
93. **C**   (Both were born on June 21, 1947.)
94. **C**   (At each distance, it's about two seconds faster than the
            backstroke for top swimmers.)
95. **A**   (He was a three-time All-American at the University of
            Illinois, and a member of the Chicago Bears for eight years.)
96. **B**   (His hundredth win made him 100-36; Dwight Gooden
            nearly equaled this record, but was 100-37.)
97. **C**
98. **C**
99. **A**
100. **C**

Answers to Chapter 11: 3-Point Questions

1. **A**   (on the West Coast)
2. **B**
3. **D**
4. **B**
5. **D**
6. **A**
7. **B**
8. **B**
9. **B**   (711 survived; 1,513 did not.)
10. **B**

11. **C**
12. **A**
13. **B**
14. **D**
15. **A**   (He was fined $150,000 and sentenced to 1,200 hours community service and two years' probation.)
16. **C**   (She was born in 1958.)
17. **C**
18. **D**
19. **B**
20. **C**
21. **D**   (The chairman's name was Roger Smith.)
22. **C**   (spoken by Princess Leia to Han Solo, referring to Luke Skywalker, in *Return of the Jedi*)
23. **B**
24. **D**
25. **B**   (Acetaminophen is a generic pain reliever. Nutrasweet is a brand of aspartame, and Sunette is a brand of acesulfame K.)
26. **A**
27. **A**   (They are owned by General Mills.)
28. **B**   (Whitey Ford had 10 World Series victories.)
29. **A**   (He appointed Lauro Cavazos as education secretary.)
30. **C**   (Trade between the countries is approximately $150 billion per year.)
31. **B**
32. **C**
33. **C**
34. **C**   (Rice is used in some American beers, however.)
35. **B**
36. **B**   (Celebrations, which followed a two-year restoration project, were held on both July 4 and on October 28, the latter being the anniversary of the dedication of the statue by President Grover Cleveland.)
37. **D**
38. **D**
39. **A**
40. **D**
41. **C**
42. **C**   (Cartwright, not Abner Doubleday, did the most to invent the game.)
43. **C**
44. **B**   (6,137 performances)

45. **A**   (He won the Masters in 1989 and 1990, and the British Open in 1987 and 1990.)
46. **B**
47. **B**
48. **C**
49. **A**
50. **D**
51. **D**
52. **A**
53. **B**
54. **B**
55. **A**
56. **C**
57. **C**
58. **A**
59. **B**
60. **B**
61. **C**
62. **A**
63. **C**
64. **D**
65. **A**
66. **A**   (It made photography affordable for most everyone for the first time.)
67. **C**
68. **D**   (in Australian slang)
69. **C**
70. **C**
71. **A**   (AT&T has roughly 2,700,000 stockholders. General Motors, with the second-highest number of stockholders, has about 1 million fewer.)
72. **D**
73. **C**
74. **A**
75. **C**
76. **B**
77. **B**
78. **A**   (*Barchester Towers* was written by Anthony Trollope.)
79. **D**   ("Halloween" is short for "All Hallows' Eve," the day before.)
80. **B**
81. **B**
82. **B**

83. **B**
84. **C**
85. **B**
86. **D**
87. **B**
88. **A**   (76%; Carter 51%, Reagan 49%, Nixon 61%; John Kennedy had the best rating ever, 79%.)
89. **A**
90. **A**
91. **A**
92. **C**
93. **A**
94. **C**
95. **B**   (In 1800, though it was not yet finished. Theodore Roosevelt took office in 1902.)
96. **C**
97. **A**
98. **D**
99. **B**
100. **C**
101. **D**   (He completed 106. Bruckner began a 10th, but never finished it.)

	1-point questions	2-point questions	3-point questions
Entertainment, Literature, and Art			
Geography and Sightseeing			
History and Demographics			
Science and Nature			
Sports and Games			
Potpourri			

	1-point questions	2-point questions	3-point questions
Entertainment, Literature, and Art			
Geography and Sightseeing			
History and Demographics			
Science and Nature			
Sports and Games			
Potpourri			

	1-point questions	2-point questions	3-point questions
Entertainment, Literature, and Art			
Geography and Sightseeing			
History and Demographics			
Science and Nature			
Sports and Games			
Potpourri			

	1-point questions	2-point questions	3-point questions
Entertainment, Literature, and Art			
Geography and Sightseeing			
History and Demographics			
Science and Nature			
Sports and Games			
Potpourri			

	1-point questions	2-point questions	3-point questions
Entertainment, Literature, and Art			
Geography and Sightseeing			
History and Demographics			
Science and Nature			
Sports and Games			
Potpourri			

	1-point questions	2-point questions	3-point questions
Entertainment, Literature, and Art			
Geography and Sightseeing			
History and Demographics			
Science and Nature			
Sports and Games			
Potpourri			